W9-AHI-265

# A Want of Vigilance

## THE BRISTOE STATION CAMPAIGN, OCTOBER 9-19, 1863

by Bill Backus and Robert Orrison

EMERGING CIVIL WAR SERIES

Chris Mackowski, *series editor*
Daniel T. Davis, *chief historian*
Kristopher D. White, *emeritus editor*

**Also part of the Emerging Civil War Series:**

# A Want of Vigilance

## THE BRISTOE STATION CAMPAIGN, OCTOBER 9-19, 1863

by Bill Backus and Robert Orrison

Savas Beatie

California

© 2015 by Bill Backus and Robert Orrison

All rights reserved. No part of this publication may be reproduced, stored in a retrieval system, or transmitted, in any form or by any means, electronic, mechanical, photocopying, recording, or otherwise, without the prior written permission of the publisher. Printed in the United States of America.

First edition, first printing

ISBN-13: 978-1-61121-300-3
eISBN: 978-1-61121-301-0

Library of Congress Control Number: 2015029294

SB

Published by
Savas Beatie LLC
989 Governor Drive, Suite 102
El Dorado Hills, California 95762
Phone: 916-941-6896
Email: sales@savasbeatie.com
Web: www.savasbeatie.com

Savas Beatie titles are available at special discounts for bulk purchases in the United States by corporations, institutions, and other organizations. For more details, please contact Special Sales, P.O. Box 4527, El Dorado Hills, CA 95762, or you may e-mail us as at sales@savasbeatie.com, or visit our website at www. savasbeatie.com for additional information.

*"No more for them the pleasing hearth shall burn,*
*Nor busy housewife ply her evening care;*
*No children run to greet their sire's return,*
*Or climb his knees, the envied kiss to share"*

*— Brig. Gen. Alexander Hays to his wife,*
*October 21, 1863*

*Dedicated to the thousands of men who came*
*to a little-known place called Bristoe and never*
*returned home. Many still lie there below the earth*
*today. May they be forgotten no more.*

# Table of Contents

# List of Maps

*Maps by Hal Jespersen*

# Acknowledgments

No one could write a book without the assistance of many friends and colleagues. First we want to thank Chris Mackowski for encouraging us on this project; without him it never would have been completed.

Thanks to Ted Savas and the staff of Savas Beatie, LLC, for the continual support of this project and the entire Emerging Civil War Series. Also thanks to our fellow Emerging Civil War authors for showing us the ropes and giving great advice.

We relied heavily on our colleagues in the field who are experts in the fall campaign of 1863. Frank Walker knows more about Civil War history in Orange than anyone else. Clark "Bud" Hall, the expert on everything Brandy Station—through his efforts a good portion of that battlefield is preserved. Mike Block, one of the experts on Culpeper County history, read several chapters and made excellent suggestions. John

George Gilmore, born into slavery in the early 1800s, lived in this house across the road from James Madison's Montpelier estate outside of Orange. He built his cabin from the remains of winter huts left behind by Confederates from the winter of 1863-64. Today, the cabin is visible from the road and marks the head of a trail that leads back to a reconstructed Confederate winter camp. (cm)

Tole helped laying out the Confederate march from Orange to Warrenton. John Pearson, John DePue, Jay Greevy, and Jimmy Price have been our partners in crime at Bristoe Battlefield and have supported this project from the beginning. Adrian Tighe guided us through some "tough" research questions. Jeff Hunt, whose manuscript on July 1863-May 1864 is an excellent addition to any library, was helpful in sharing sources and making suggestions to our manuscript. Jim Burgess has been a supporter and advocate of preserving the Bristoe Station battlefield way before anyone else thought about it. Phil Greenwalt, Patricia Rich, and Dan Welch assisted with modern photos.

Finally, Mike Miller not only read over the manuscript and provided the foreword, but also encouraged us to do this project. Mike did a lot of the research on Bristoe Station for the interpretive markers and assisted us finishing that project.

We apologize for anyone we have not mentioned.
— *Rob Orrison and Bill Backus*

I want to thank my parents for encouraging my love of history and encouraging me to make it my profession. To my wife for putting up with being dragged to Civil War sites and allowing me the freedom to take trips for research and share my love of history with others. To my in-laws for watching our son on the many occasions where I needed to work on this project—without them, this would never have been possible. To my good friend and battlefield partner, Matt Atkinson—no one tells the story of the Civil War better than Matt.

Thanks to co author and friend Bill Backus for being one of the best researchers I

Two cannons still stand vigil near the Bristoe Station Battlefield Heritage Park visitor center. (cm)

know and for putting up with my constant harassment during this project. Our work at Bristoe, I think, is something to be proud of.

Finally to my son Carter, for reminding me why it's important to preserve and tell the story of our collective past. I hope he grows up to appreciate history and learn from it to build a better future for us all.
— *Rob Orrison*

PHOTO CREDITS: **Mike Block (mb); Gettysburg National Military Park (gnmp); Phillip Greenwalt (pg); Harper's Weekly (hw); Library of Congress (loc); Chris Mackowski (cm); MOLLUS (mls); Rob Orrison (ro); Prince William County (pwc); Patricia Rich (pr); Virginia Historical Society (vhs); Dan Welch (dw)**

*For the Emerging Civil War Series*

Theodore P. Savas, publisher
Chris Mackowski, series editor
Daniel T. Davis, chief historian
Sarah Keeney, editorial consultant
Kristopher D. White, emeritus editor and co-founder

Design and layout by Levi Trimble
Maps by Hal Jespersen

# Touring the Battlefields

During the Bristoe Station campaign, the armies maneuvered over large swaths of central Virginia. This book will condense the campaign and emphasize the highlights. It will cover a large area geographically. Route 29 will serve as the major highway that will be the basis for most of the driving. Many of the tour stops will use historic roadways and take you through many scenic areas of this part of Virginia.

As always, be safe, as Route 29 is a busy road and most of the other historic roads used in the tour are rural, winding byways.

The tour stops follow the campaign chronologically. The only established publicly accessible battlefield spaces are at Brandy Station and Bristoe Station.

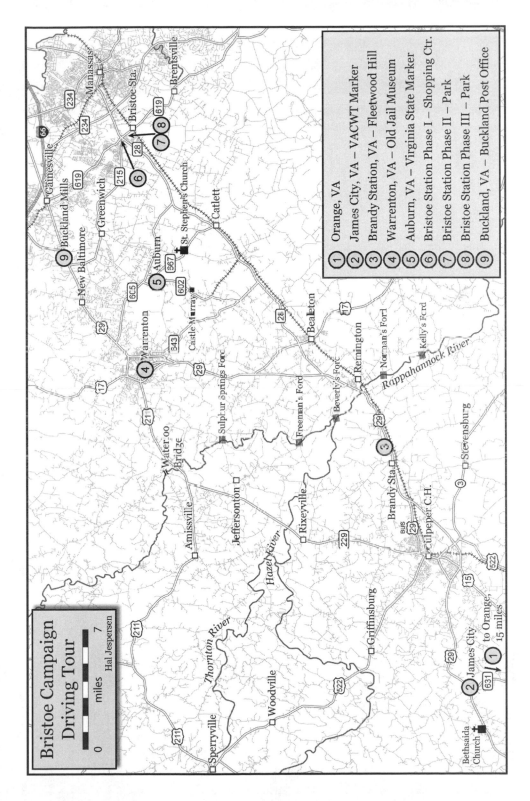

Bristoe Campaign
Driving Tour

0    miles    7

Hal Jespersen

1. Orange, VA
2. James City, VA – VACWT Marker
3. Brandy Station, VA – Fleetwood Hill
4. Warrenton, VA – Old Jail Museum
5. Auburn, VA – Virginia State Marker
6. Bristoe Station Phase I – Shopping Ctr.
7. Bristoe Station Phase II – Park
8. Bristoe Station Phase III – Park
9. Buckland, VA – Buckland Post Office

Few gravestones remain on Bristoe's only identified cemetery. (cm)

# Foreword

BY J. MICHAEL MILLER

In all of my Civil War ramblings, I have only been thrown off of two battlefields: one shall remain nameless, the other was Bristoe Station. Perhaps this incident ignited my stubborn mind to uncover what really happened on this forbidden battlefield, but it also created a determination to help preserve this hallowed ground.

This image of the Orange and Alexandria Railroad at Bristoe Station shows the destruction of the rail line by the Confederates after the battle of Bristoe Station. (loc)

My first great impressions of Bristoe, other than from books, came when the local landowners invited me to walk the ground, with the intent of bringing notice to the importance of the battlefield, which was threatened by the potential placement of a landfill. Accompanied by Doug Harvey, then head of the Manassas Museum, I was able to walk the ground while it was still in pristine condition, see the 1861 burial grounds with stones still in place, and feel the presence of the soldiers on both sides who fought and died there.

The result of the walk? I was now captivated by

the Bristoe Battlefield, which has become a lifelong fascination, extending now over almost thirty years.

I first presented a talk about Bristoe on October 15, 1988—marking the 125th Anniversary of the battle—along with Doug Harvey and William D. Henderson, author of The Road to Bristoe Station, the first real study of the campaign. The irony of the event was that we could not hold the event on the battlefield because the landowners withheld permission. So, the presentations were done at the Brentsville Historic District. The turnout was modest, but ignited a spark in many of the local populace, which began to realize with heartfelt emotion the historical importance of their land.

This talk and a brief but poignant article on the battle, titled "Bristoe Station, Prince William County's Forgotten Battlefield," launched me forever into preserving this battleground. I soon found myself making presentations to locals groups as well as the Virginia Department of Historic Resources, and I kindled friendships with Annie Synder and Linda McCarthy of the Save the Battlefield Coalition and other like-minded folks determined to save this battlefield. No matter how much we tried over the years, the obstacles in our way seemed insurmountable and Bristoe seemed doomed.

So many times over the intervening years, saving the battlefield seemed a hopeless exercise, lost unnoticed beneath the fame of other Civil War sites that were more famous. Finally, a miracle occurred when the Bristoe Station Battlefield Heritage Park was acquired

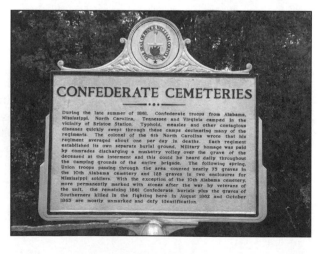

Bristoe Station also has a story rooted in 1861, when Confederates established an encampment here after the battle of First Manassas. During several months, nearly 1,000 men died due to disease. Most of the cemeteries are lost to history. (loc)

by Prince William County from the Civil War Trust in 2006. In working with the county and Civil War Trust, I was able to identify the significant features of the park, including the Confederate cemeteries, and then lay out the first interpretive trail system for the park, which included Camp Jones from 1861 and portions of the 1862 Kettle Run battlefield. Correcting the location of the August 1862 battle away from Kettle Run itself will always stand as a source of pride.

In working with the county during this process, I first met Rob Orrison, who was assigned by Prince William County to interpret the site. While preserving a battlefield takes a village of people, taking that battlefield to the next level of interpretation requires someone with vision and the energy to bring that visualization to actuality. Admirably, Rob has assumed that role, quietly and confidently. The publication of his book reflects a culmination of farsightedness matched with experience, along with many miles of walking this battlefield. He represents the new generation of historians who have stepped forward to safeguard our battlefields. Enjoy the words that Rob has written, and know something of the struggle for this battlefield to simply exist.

Bristoe is a battlefield that is meant for walking. You cannot understand what happened here by sitting in your car, reading signs, or listening to an audio tour. Visitors can now walk these trails accompanied by a volunteer guide and experience Bristoe up close and personal— where years ago there was no possibility of this happening. Rob is a huge part of this success, and I look to a future of more of his accomplishments on this battlefield. This book marks a new level of understanding for Civil War scholars and the general public alike, continuing to make Bristoe one of the great success stories of Civil War battlefield preservation.

J. MICHAEL MILLER *is Special Projects Historian, World War I at the Marine Corps History Division. He has served more than 30 years working in the Marine Corps historical program, including director of the Marine Corps Archives. He has published books and articles on several Civil War battles, including the Battle of North Anna and Bristoe Station.*

"Twice baptized in blood for
Liberty's sake, it will be a place
to which in after times
pilgrimages will be made
by those who reverence the
glorious, though suffering, past."

— *Chaplain, Joseph Hopkins Twichell,
71st New York Infantry,
November 1, 1863,
visiting the Bristoe Station battlefields.*

# *Prologue*

BY ROB ORRISON

In 1999, a good friend and history colleague of mine and I were out exploring little-known Civil War battlefields. I was living in Fairfax, so we drove around the northern Virginia area seeing sites that only the "hardcore" Civil War buffs would seek out—mostly places with no signs, no interpretation, and no preserved space.

Our drive took us south of Manassas to a place called Bristow. We had both heard of a Bristoe Station, but this was spelled differently. Was this the same place? We drove down the two-lane road to a railroad crossing. As we walked along the rail line, we recognized the strength of the embankment. All we knew about Bristoe was that a fool-hearty attack by the Confederates against Federal troops behind a rail embankment like this one ended in a bloody repulse.

As we stood there, we tried to dig through our Lee's Lieutenants by favorite author Douglas Southall Freeman. We figured that the Confederate attack surely came from the south. But before we could read the chapter on Bristoe Station, railroad security arrived and asked us to move on. Sadly, we got in our cars and drove to the next little-known battlefield, never knowing the true story of Bristoe Station.

This story exemplifies the battle of Bristoe Station: much forgotten and misunderstood. Until recently, only one book and a few articles highlighted this often-overlooked Civil War campaign. Most historians skip over the fall of 1863 entirely—going from Gettysburg to Chickamauga or the Wilderness. Most people believed that after Gettysburg, Lee went south

After Hill's Carolinians began their wheel towards the railroad tracks, Warren's skirmishers retreated to this farm road by the railroad. (pg)

and stayed there until attacked by Lt. Gen. Ulysses S. Grant in 1864.

Of course, that is not true. History—specifically Civil War history—is always more complicated than the way it's taught and understood.

In October 1863, the Army of Northern Virginia found itself again on the offensive, pushing back the Army of the Potomac all the way to Centreville. The actions of that campaign had a direct impact on the outcome of the war.

Lee's failure in the campaign proved that his leadership and army were much weakened by Gettysburg and would never again be the effective military force it used to be. Meade's inability to keep Lee from nonetheless pushing him back to the outskirts of Washington, D.C., led Lincoln to start looking for a new commander to deal with the Army of Northern Virginia. Meade proved during the Bristoe Station campaign that he was just not the aggressive general to take the war to Lee.

I myself failed to understand these circumstances . . . to understand that, though light in casualties, the men from the North Carolina brigade of Brig. Gen. John Cooke suffered some of the heaviest casualties of any brigade during the war . . . to understand that the campaign as a whole was intricate and covered a large swatch of land from Orange to Centreville.

Lee's plan for maneuver was excellent, and Meade's ability to thwart each of Lee's moves masterful.

I even failed to understand the battlefield that day my friend and I visited. We had the Confederates attacking the railroad embankment from the south—which was wrong. The Confederates attacked from the north. That's an embarrassing admission from two guys who think they know a lot about the Civil War!

The ending of this story is a fitting one. Like so many coincidences in one's life, 10 years after my visit to Bristow, I received a job with Prince William County. One of my responsibilities would be to oversee the interpretation and development of a new battlefield park: Bristoe Station.

# The Campaign

## CHAPTER ONE
### OCTOBER 1863

Confederate Gen. Robert E. Lee climbed Clarks' Mountain in central Virginia and looked over the large Federal army before him. This was not the first time during the war Lee had looked out from the popular Confederate signal post, but this time was different. Five months previous, his trusted "right arm," Lt. Gen. Thomas "Stonewall" Jackson, was mortally wounded at Chancellorsville. His "war horse," Lt. Gen. James Longstreet, was now with Gen. Braxton Bragg in northern Georgia and had contributed to the Confederate victory at Chickamauga. His two present corps commanders, Lt. Gen. Richard Ewell and Lt. Gen. A. P. Hill, were proven division commanders, but had been less than ideal at the corps level.

Also, his army was different. The spring and summer campaign that had been full of so much promise had ended on the fields of Gettysburg in early July. The Army of Northern Virginia suffered heavy losses in men and especially in leaders. Times had been so tough after Gettysburg that Lee offered his resignation to Confederate President Jefferson Davis. Lee's health was also weakened (and historians now know he probably suffered a mild heart attack that summer).

With all of this on his mind, Lee looked out over the Army of the Potomac in Culpeper County, determined to find a way to retake the initiative. Lee believed victory could only be achieved if the Confederates held the initiative. Lee made his intentions known to President Davis, stating, "If General Meade does not move, I wish to attack him."

The Federal army that Lee looked over was also

**Throughout the fall and winter 1863-1864, many of the Confederate high command, including Gen. R. E. Lee, worshipped at St. Thomas Church in Orange. (cm)**

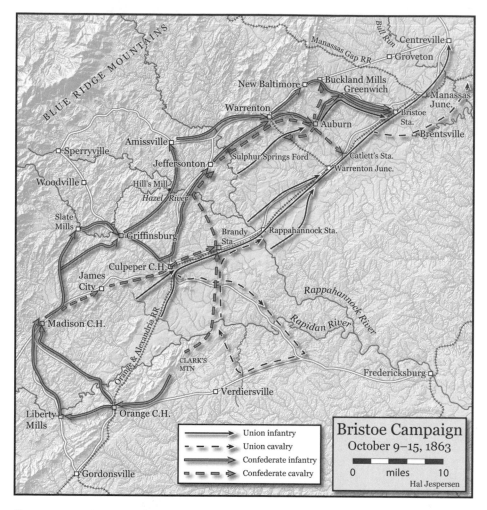

**BRISTOE CAMPAIGN**—The Bristoe campaign covered a large swath of central Virginia. The armies fought over this area continuously the entire war, due mainly to the importance of the Orange and Alexandria Railroad and two natural defensive barriers, the Rappahannock and Rapidan Rivers.

not the same Army of the Potomac it had been at Gettysburg. In victory, they had suffered heavily as well, and many of its recent reinforcements were new draftees and substitutes of questionable quality. Maj. General George Meade, new to command at Gettysburg, was still trying to prove himself to his direct superior, Maj. Gen. Henry Halleck, and to the Lincoln administration. After Gettysburg, Meade had frustrated his superiors with his perceived lack of aggression in pursuing the retreating Confederates.

With the Confederate victory in northern Georgia at Chickamauga, Meade was forced to send two of his corps west. On September 24, the XI and XII corps, totaling 18,00 men, were shipped away. Many of the men remaining with Meade were recent conscripts, and no one knew how they would perform. Both sides had worn-out cavalry, with broken mounts and weary

riders. This cavalry would play a significant role in the upcoming campaign.

While the Union war effort was buoyed by the multiple victories in the summer of 1863, resentment of the Lincoln administration's handling of the war still simmered in the Northern electorate. The Federal draft was met with resistance all over the North, with the most famous being the New York City draft riots. On top of this, the anti-war Copperhead movement was gaining such support that the Democratic nominee for governor in Ohio, Clement Vallandigham, was campaigning in exile in Canada after being thrown out of the country for his strong anti-Lincoln views. While Vallandigham was the most prominent member of the anti-war faction running for office that fall, he was not the only one. Horatio Seymour was running for the governorship of New York on an anti-Lincoln platform as well. With anti-war sentiment consolidating in time for the fall elections, the Union war effort could still be defeated militarily if the Confederate army could convince Northern voters that the Southerners would continue to fight.

Knowing the importance of a fall campaign, Meade, ever cautious, felt pressure to move against Lee in Virginia so Lee could not reinforce Bragg's army in the west at Chattanooga. Though Lee's army was reduced by one corps, Meade still believed Lee's army numbered nearly 70,000 — he had no way to know Lee's returns on September 30 only showed 55,000 men present—while Meade's Army of the Potomac still held a numeral advantage at 76,000.

Meade's inaction in Culpeper that fall led Lee to

**Clark's Mountain was a prominent ridge along the Rapidan River. It was used by Lee several times throughout the war as a command post and signal station. (ro)**

**During the Bristoe campaign, Lee heavily relied on Lt. Gen. Richard Ewell, who still stung from criticism over his performance at Gettysburg. (loc)**

**Commander of the Army of the Potomac since June, Maj. Gen. George Meade was not aggressive enough after Gettysburg for Halleck or Lincoln. (loc)**

**Maj. Gen. Henry Halleck kept the pressure on Meade to fight Lee throughout the fall of 1863. His frustrations and testy relationship with Meade would add to Lincoln's stress. (loc)**

seize the initiative and determine if he could outwit his adversary.

The strategy Lee envisioned was one not much different from a strategy the Federals would use the following summer: Lee wanted Confederate forces in the east to move in concert. Movements on the various fronts would then keep the enemy from reinforcing threatened points.

Lee sought permission from Jefferson Davis to conduct the campaign. With Longstreet and Bragg keeping the Federals busy in Tennessee, Lee wrote later that he wanted to "prevent [Meade] from detaching reinforcements to Rosecrans."

Lee also knew that Meade had lost two of his corps and so believed now was the best time to strike. He was still outnumbered, but that had never been a hindrance for the aggressive commander before.

Meeting with his commanders and staff, he began formulating his overall campaign strategy.

\* \* \*

The army Lee sought to strike was spread out along the northern bank of the Rapidan River from Germanna Ford in the east to Rapidan Station and then along the northern bank of the Robertson River, a branch of the Rapidan. Meade's headquarters were at the Wallach house in Culpeper with signal stations at Mount Pony, Cedar Mountain, and Thorofare Mountain.

To Meade's advantage, the Federals recently broken the Confederate semaphore code and were able to read all the Confederate communications via their signal stations. With cavalry covering his flanks, Meade began using his horsemen to probe for weaknesses in the Confederate lines. Meade was still receiving pressure from Washington to attack Lee and planned to make an offensive of his own.

The Army of the Potomac consisted of five infantry corps with a very different command structure since the summer. The I Corps was commanded by Maj. Gen. John Newton, who replaced the popular John Reynolds, killed at Gettysburg. Newton was unproven at corps command. The II Corps also had a new commander, Maj. Gen. Gouverneur Warren, made famous at Gettysburg for his reconnaissance at Little Round Top. Warren replaced Maj. Gen. Winfield Hancock while Hancock recovered from a wound he suffered at Gettysburg. Warren was an able engineer, but he previously commanded only a small brigade of infantry. The III Corps, previously led by the tenacious Dan Sickles, was now led by Maj. Gen. William French. Referred to as "old blinky" because of an eye tick, French previously served as a division commander and a district commander. Major General George Sykes was one of Meade's most seasoned corps commanders that fall. Sykes, a Regular Army officer, led Meade's old V Corps since Meade's promotion to army commander. Finally, the VI Corps was led by probably the best corps commander in the Federal army, Maj. Gen. John Sedgwick, a proven fighter and proven leader. Promoted to corps command early in 1863, "Uncle John" was beloved by his men.

The Federal cavalry was under Maj. Gen. Alfred Pleasonton, whose cavalry earned new respect from their foe during the Gettysburg campaign. Broken into three divisions, Pleasonton had three experienced commanders. Brigadier General John Buford, one of the heroes of Gettysburg, led the First Division. Brigadier General David Gregg, leader of the Second Division, also handled himself and his men well at Gettysburg, fighting off Stuart's attacks on July 3. Finally, Brig. Gen. Judson Kilpatrick commanded the Third Division. Considered by many to be a reckless commander, Kilpatrick was arrogant and known for his aggressive demeanor.

From his headquarters at the Wallach house in Culpeper, Meade looked for a way to take the offensive against the entrenched Confederates on the south bank of the Rapidan.

After Gettysburg, Gen. Robert E. Lee offered his resignation to President Jefferson Davis. Davis refused, and Lee carried on. He dealt with ill health throughout the Bristoe campaign. (loc)

\*   \*   \*

Lee sought to replicate his flanking maneuvers of the summer of 1862, when the Confederates out-flanked Gen. John Pope's army along the Rapidan and then the Rappahannock rivers. However, Lee wanted the new movement to involve all the forces in Virginia. He would order the available Confederate forces in western Virginia under Maj. Gen. Sam Jones and in the Shenandoah Valley under Maj. Gen. John Imboden to also move northward. This, he hoped, would keep Federal forces in those regions engaged and keep them from joining Meade. Lee wrote to Jones on October 9: "I think it is very important that our troops everywhere should advance upon the enemy."

Also, this campaign would be one of maneuver, and the other forces moving through western Virginia

**This sketch by Alfred Waud of the Federal signal station on Mount Pony shows Clark Mountain in the distance.** (loc)

might give the Federals the impression that Lee was heading back to the Shenandoah Valley for another possible invasion of Maryland.

As he laid out his offensive at his headquarters at the Rogers farm near Orange, Lee said he would rely heavily on Maj. Gen. J. E. B. Stuart's cavalry to screen his army's movement and to keep the Federals in place along the Rapidan. The movement would require secrecy and illusion. Stuart was perfect for this, and he sought to prepare his men for the task. Stuart would lead a division personally because one of his division commanders, Maj. Gen. Wade Hampton, was still recovering from wounds suffered at Gettysburg.

The infantry, meanwhile, would leave their camps and take concealed roads to the west. The destination was Culpeper Courthouse and the rear of the Army of the Potomac. Lee had received reports that Meade was no longer in force there on his western flank near Stonehouse Mountain and that Federals might be vulnerable to just such a flanking maneuver. If Lee could not gain Meade's rear, he would at least regain the initiative and possibly catch Meade in an error during his maneuvering as he tried to counter the Confederate move.

It was time, Lee decided, to make something happen.

JJ 2
LEE'S
HEADQUARTERS

Half a mile west, at the Rogers farm called Middle Hill. Gen. Robert E. Lee kept his headquarters from Dec. 1863 to May 1864. His Army of Northern Virginia, in winter camp, guarded the south side of the Rapidan River from the vicinity of Liberty Mills in Somerset east to Morton's Ford. While Lee strove to reinforce and resupply his depleted ranks, across the river in Culpeper County Lt. Gen. Ulysses S. Grant and Maj. Gen. George G. Meade trained and strengthened the Army of the Potomac for the spring campaign. On 4 May 1864, the Wilderness campaign began anew.

DEPARTMENT OF HISTORIC RESOURCES, 1998

East of Orange on the Rogers farm, Lee located his headquarters in the fall and winter of 1863. The farm was located south of modern day Rt. 20. (cm)

*At the Town of Orange*

The town of Orange, strategically located in central Virginia south of the Rapidan River and astride the Orange and Alexandria Railroad, saw little fighting during the war. The town was the scene of many encampments and troop movements, though. When Lee's men arrived here in early September, their duty was to protect the railroad and the southern bank of the Rapidan River. The Army of Northern Virginia built significant earthworks guarding the various fords and approaches.

Clarks' Mountain, located a few miles northeast of Orange, served throughout the war as a significant observation post for the Confederates. Today, it can be easily identified by the various communication towers on its summit. Most of it is private property, though portions can be accessed by a public road to obtain the view that Lee had in 1863.

Just east of Orange was the Rogers farm, where Lee set up his headquarters before and after the Bristoe campaign. Today, a state marker along Rt. 20 east of Orange marks the nearby location, which is now on private property.

GPS: N 38.244861 W 78.109857

**The encampments of Brig. Gen. Samuel McGowan's brigade are recreated at James Madison's Montpelier in a special Civil War exhibit.** (cm)

In downtown Orange, St. Thomas Episcopal Church was frequented by the officers of the Army of Northern Virginia, including Lee himself. Today, the church marks the pew where—legend has it—Lee preferred to sit. During late summer and early fall of 1863, many soldiers on both sides wrote of a religious revival sweeping the armies. The church was also used at various times as a hospital throughout the war.

South of downtown Orange along Rt. 15 is Mayhurst, today a bed and breakfast. Here is where Lt. Gen. A. P. Hill had his headquarters from the fall of 1863 through the spring of 1864.

Finally, located west of town near Montpelier— the home of James Madison and current historic house museum—is the location of Brig. Gen. Samuel McGowan's South Carolina brigade winter encampments. Here several representative winter huts are recreated to give visitors an example of the large Confederate camps that existed in Orange County during the winter of 1863. Montpelier maintains an access road to the recreated Confederate camp and the Gilmore Cabin on the right side of the highway, just past Montpelier's entrance.

# ➡ To Stop 2

Take Rt. 20 west from Orange. You will pass by Montpelier, and you may be interested in stopping at the Civil War winter encampment exhibit on the right side of the road across from the Montpelier main entrance.

Beyond, continue on Rt. 20 and take a right onto Rt. 231 (Blue Ridge Tnpk.). Follow Rt. 231 to Rt. 29 east into Madison. Along this route you will pass the Jack's Shop battlefield; a Civil War Trails sign on the left side of the road just after the village of Rochelle marks the area. This cavalry battle was fought in September 1863.

Continue approximately eight miles past Madison to Leon (historically James City). The Virginia Civil War Trails marker and parking lot is on the right side of the highway.

GPS: N 38.437633, W 78.137937

Built in 1860, Hill and his staff set up their headquarters in the yard of Mayhurst during the fall and winter of 1863. Today the home serves as a bed and breakfast in Orange. (ro)

Alfred Waud drew many sketches during the 1863 fall campaign, including this signal tower on a house in Culpeper. (loc)

# This Month Won't Pass Away Without a Battle

## CHAPTER TWO
### OCTOBER 8 –10, 1863

On October 8, Lee ordered his quartermasters and pioneers to prepare for the advance, and he evacuated most of his hospitalized men out of Orange via railroad to Gordonsville. J. E. B. Stuart with Hampton's division would lead the advance and screen the infantry. Stuart would also seek out and silence the troublesome Federal signal station atop Thorofare Mountain.

Lee's plan for the campaign was simple. He intended to get around the Federal flank or rear and fight a battle on his terms or at least force Meade north of the Rappahannock River. Much of his 1862 Second Manassas campaign strategy would be replicated: make the Federal army move northward while, in the meantime, trying to find an advantageous opportunity to attack them while in motion.

The army would march as two wings. The corps under Lt. Gen. A. P. Hill would march on a wider, more western arc while Lt. Gen. Richard Ewell's corps would take a more direct route. Both wings would march to Madison Courthouse, then on to a point west or to the rear of Culpeper and Meade's army.

Maj. General Fitz Lee's cavalry division, with an infantry brigade under the temporary command of Col. Thomas Garrett, would be left behind to fill the old Rapidan entrenchments and watch the various fords. Their role was to maintain a Confederate presence and attempt to deceive the Federals about the army's general movement west and north. They also had to make sure the Federals would not swing southward and attack the rear of the moving Confederate army.

Lee, who was suffering a bout of rheumatism,

**Built in 1828, the Madison Country Courthouse witnessed the Army of Northern Virginia on October 9 and 10. Upon arriving in Madison, most Confederates had no idea where they would head next. (ro)**

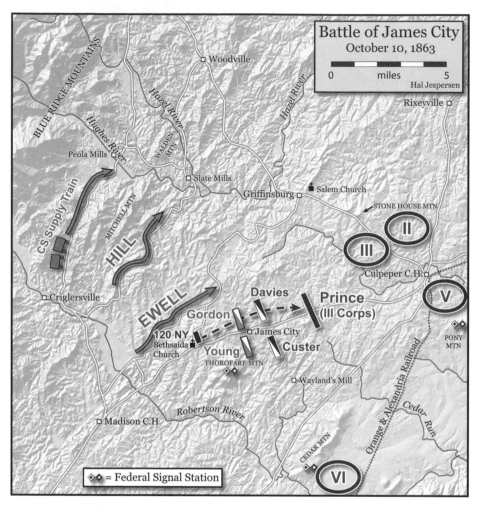

**BATTLE OF JAMES CITY**—On the morning of October 10, Confederate cavalry under Maj. Gen. Stuart screened the Confederate infantry eastward from Madison Courthouse toward James City. Near James City, Stuart ran into elements of Federal cavalry under Brig. Gen. George Custer and Brig. Gen. Henry Davies. After a brisk fight, the Federal cavalry pulled back near infantry support under Brig. Gen. Henry Prince. This, in turn, allowed the Confederate infantry columns to march northeast from Madison Courthouse, their destination unknown to Federal scouts.

was in great pain and rode in a wagon instead of on horseback. He attached himself to Ewell's corps—the one most likely to come into contact with the Army of the Potomac.

Lee wanted there to be an element of surprise, but the newspapers in Richmond were already reporting his northward movement before it even began. The newspaper reports "are injurious to us," Lee wrote to Confederate Secretary of War James Seddon. "[W]e have difficulties enough to overcome interposed by our enemies, without having them augmented by our friends."

As Confederate signalmen sent messages back and forth to the various commanders, they were being watched by their counterparts. The Federal signal stations at Thorofare Mountain, Cedar Mountain, and Mount Pony had all been tasked with watching the Confederate movements. This allowed the Federals to be aware of the Confederate movement before it began, although Meade would be left guessing if this new movement was an offensive or a movement south.

On October 8, Confederate infantry began shifting to the various fords along the Rapidan River near Orange. Ewell's corps, positioned east of Orange near Morton and Raccoon Fords, moved west to new camps near Barnett's Ford northwest of Orange. Hill's corps moved from their camps around Orange and moved west near Cave's Ford.

The Confederate soldiers knew they were probably opening another campaign. As Stanley Russell of the 13th Virginia observed, "I do not think this month will pass away without a battle."

Morale ran high and most men were excited to be on the move again. "[W]e were in fit shape for a rift with Meade," wrote William Long, "and keen to get even with him for the attack we met at Gettysburg."

*     *     *

On the early morning of October 9, columns of Confederates began to cross the Rapidan. Hill's corps led the way, crossing at Cave's Ford with Ewell's men crossing at Barnett's Ford. Lee ordered his men to travel back roads to avoid detection by the Federal signal stations. The march followed "no particular road" and avoided marching over hills through dusty roads—all to provide the highest privacy possible for Lee's march.

As much as Lee tried to keep his movement secret, though, Federal pickets reported the activity. Also, with the help of well-placed spies and the cracking of the Confederate semaphore code, Meade was aware of the Confederate movement. The problem Meade was having, though, was where was Lee going? Was it a feint, or was it a retrograde movement southward?

Meade would rely on his cavalry to bring him more intelligence. He also decided to push across the Rapidan to see if that would give him a clearer picture. Meade could either identify Lee's intentions or possibly attack him while the Confederates moved toward Richmond.

Maj. Gen. J. E. B. Stuart saw
an opportunity in the fall 1863
to redeem his name from his
perceived failures during the
Gettysburg campaign. His
cavalry effectively provided
Lee information and screened
the infantry. (loc)

Crossing the river would also possibly allow Meade to change his base of supply from the Orange and Alexandria (O&A) Railroad to Fredericksburg. Meade did not trust the railroad to be reliable with constant enemy raids against it and its ability to move large amounts of supplies. In Fredericksburg, he could use the Potomac and Rappahannock rivers, which the Federals fully controlled. This was something he had proposed to his superiors, but neither Halleck nor Lincoln would agree to his moving out of central Virginia. To them, Meade's goal was Lee's army, and Lee was located in central Virginia, not near Fredericksburg.

To start his move, Meade ordered Brigadier General Buford's cavalry division across the river at Germanna Ford and then moved his I, V, and VI corps into supporting distance. Buford, with the possible help of the I Corps, would move west once the infantry also crossed at Germanna. That would, in turn, uncovered Morton's Ford and allow the V and VI corps to cross to the south side of the river.

At noon on October 10, Buford's cavalry crossed the Rapidan and began moving upstream toward Morton's Ford. They met very little resistance, as most of the Confederates were miles away marching in the opposite direction towards Madison Courthouse.

By that point, Confederate cavalry had already picked a fight.

Early on October 10, Stuart's cavalry division attacked a Federal cavalry division under Brig. Gen. Judson Kilpatrick, located around the village of James City, halfway between Culpeper and Madison. Kilpatrick's cavalry had been ordered by Meade to scout west of Culpeper, just in case Lee was moving on the Federal western flank.

Stuart's mission was to screen the moving infantry from the Federal cavalry. To do so, he needed to push the Federal cavalry eastward to allow Lee's columns to clear the Robinson River and move northward and thus around Meade's army centered along the Rapidan River and Culpeper.

Two of Stuart's brigades—those of Col. Pierce Young and Brig. Gen. James Gordon—pushed aside the Federal cavalry pickets along the Robinson. In response, Kilpatrick called for infantry support from the Federal III Corps under Maj. Gen. William French, who assigned Brig. Gen. Henry Prince's division to support the cavalry.

As part of that support, the 120th New York

infantry, under the command of Capt. Abram Lockwood, was posted near Bethsaida Church. As the Confederates pushed eastward, they came upon Lockwood's 211 infantrymen. Lockwood ordered his outnumbered regiment to stand their ground. Stuart ordered Gordon's brigade to attack the New Yorkers head on while Young's brigade attacked their flank.

The outcome was predictable: after firing a few shots, the New Yorkers broke. Of the 211 men who lined up that morning, nearly 115 were casualties, mostly captured.

After dealing with the 120th New York, Stuart's cavalry approached the main Federal cavalry line around James City. With this movement, Federals abandoned their signal station on the summit of Thorofare Mountain. They had played an integral part in informing Meade of Lee's westward flank movement, but were now about to be behind enemy lines.

As Stuart's cavalry pushed on to James City, Kilpatrick's men pulled back through town to a ridge on the opposite side of Crooked Run. Kilpatrick called on Prince's division for support, but Prince was reluctant to assist. This would be the first of many misgivings about Prince in the fall campaign.

Realizing he was on his own, Kilpatrick positioned Brig. Gen. George Custer's brigade on the left and Col. Henry Davies's brigade on the right. Both sides called for their artillery and soon a heavy exchange took place. Stuart, keeping in mind his overall objective of screening the infantry, did not press any further. He was content in allowing his skirmishers to engage the enemy's skirmishers and to participate in a long-range artillery duel.

However, men of the 5th Michigan Cavalry began taking heavy fire from Capt. James Hart's horse artillery and decided to drive off the enemy gun battery. As men from the 5th Michigan charged, the 1st South Carolina Cavalry, positioned to support the Confederate artillery, fired a volley along with a round from Hart's guns. The Wolverines quickly turned back.

Kilpatrick made no other effort to force the issue.

As one Confederate wrote, "a spectator would have said that the opponents were afraid of each other," but Stuart was playing his role perfectly in Lee's overall campaign strategy.

During a lull in the artillery firing, Stuart and his staff laid down on the ground with their

Brig. Gen. Judson Kilpatrick's cavalry division found itself very busy during the Bristoe Campaign. Kilpatrick's cavalry provided Meade limited information on Lee's movements in early October. (loc)

**Brig. Gen. Pierce Young led Wade Hampton's Division while Hampton recovered from wounds suffered at Gettysburg. He gained Stuart's respect during the Bristoe Campaign.** (loc)

headquarters flag nearby. Soon the flag and the collection of men near it attracted the attention of a Federal gun crew. Men saw a white puff of smoke from the once-quiet artillery, and a shot whistled toward the group, landing in the ground and exploding. Though no one was hurt, Confederate staff officer John Esten Cooke wrote he was "covered in dirt where he lay . . . striking within three or four feet of his head, the incident was highly pleasing." Soon Stuart and his staff scattered to safer locations.

The night of the 10th found Stuart's cavalry screen holding James City and moving northward cross-country to Griffinsburg. Lee's infantry, after an arduous march, spread out over the Blue Ridge foothills. Hill's column, marching on the wide arc, settled near the area of Slate Mills; Ewell's men, accompanied by Lee, encamped west of Griffinsburg on the Sperryville-Culpeper Road.

The Confederate infantry and cavalry on his western flank convinced Meade to abandon Culpeper on the morning of October 11. He could not risk holding the Rapidan if Lee was moving to his right and rear. Orders were sent to all the infantry and cavalry to move northward and look out towards Sperryville for a possible Confederate attack.

Unfortunately for the Federal cavalrymen under Buford, that order meant they were on their own south of the Rapidan.

*At James City*

James City, modern day Leon, was founded early in the 19th century as a stop on a popular stage route. Many of the surviving buildings were present during the Civil War.

In 1863, there were 100 residents in town, which found itself in between the opposing lines of Confederate and Federal cavalry. The main Confederate line began to the west near the Prince Michel Winery and pushed on to the hills around James City. The Federals slowly fell back to a position located on the hills east of James City above Crooked Run (modern day Rt. 29 crosses Crooked Run just east of James City).

Hampton's division of cavalry under Stuart would leave the area around James City and screen the

infantry northward. After the fighting here at James City, most of the Federal infantry and cavalry pulled back to the area of Culpeper.

The view from Kilpatrick's position in the afternoon of October 10. Stuart's line was on the ridge on the other side of the Crooked Run. Thorofare Mountain looms in the background. (m)

## ➤ To Stop 3

A short drive down Leon Road will afford a great view of Thorofare Mountain, the location of the Federal signal station that was the objective of J. E. B. Stuart's cavalry in the early morning of October 10.

Nearby, modern Bethsaida Church stands on its wartime location. Here, the 120th New York under Capt. Abram Lockwood was overwhelmed. Picketing in front, Lockwood adhered to his orders to stand his ground when two Confederate cavalry brigades attacked. "[T]he enemy advanced in heavy force, attacking both flanks and in my front," Lockwood wrote afterwards. The 120th New York suffered 115 casualties. To visit Bethsaida Church, take Rt. 29 west and turn right on Tibbs Shop Road. Once on Tibbs Shop Road, take a right on Ridgeview Road and the church will immediately be on your right.

Eight miles west of James City is Madison, where Confederate infantry encamped on the night of October 9. From there, A. P. Hill's corps took back roads northward and reached the area around Slate Mills on the night of October 10. Richard Ewell's corps marched northward from Madison and camped near Boston, VA, west of Culpeper, on the evening of October 10.

Standing in front of the Wallach House, Commanders of the Army of the Potomac, Gouverneur K. Warren, William H. French, George G. Meade, Henry J. Hunt, Andrew A. Humphreys and George Sykes in September 1863. (loc)

*Turn right onto Route 29 and continue northward for 16 miles to Brandy Station. Turn left onto Alanthus Road and make your immediate right onto Fleetwood Heights Road. One mile on the right will be a turn off and a UDC marker for Fleetwood Hill.*

GPS: N 38.509791, W 77.879079

OPPOSITE: Once a bustling crossroads town, today much of James City still stands hidden on private property. The town found itself in between Stuart and Kilpatrick on October 10. (cm)

# "A Wild and Exciting Scene"

## CHAPTER THREE
### CULPEPER-BRANDY STATION,
### OCTOBER 11, 1863

As Confederate infantry began moving northward and Meade was reacting, Buford's cavalry division found itself south of the Rapidan River. Worse, his promised support was moving in the opposite direction towards the Rappahannock River. With Buford were the two brigades of cavalry under Col. George Chapman and Col. Thomas Devin—hardened veterans under arguably the best Federal cavalryman.

Lee, attempting to create the illusion that he was still in force along the Rapidan, left behind the infantry brigade of Col. T. M. Garrett and the cavalry division of Maj. Gen. Fitz Lee. Their objective was to guard the rear of the Army of Northern Virginia as it moved west then north and keep the Federals busy thinking that Lee was still below the Rapidan. With Fitz Lee were the cavalry brigades of Brig. Gen. Lunsford Lomax and Brig. Gen. John Chambliss, and Wickham's brigade, commanded by Col. Thomas Owen.

When scouts brought Fitz Lee word about Buford's position on the southern side of the Rapidan, the cavalryman put his men in motion the night of October 10.

Buford spent that night near Morton's Ford nervously awaiting his promised infantry support from the I Corps. Up to this point, his movement had been simple and uneventful. Finally, at 7 a.m. Buford learned of the change of plans: Meade was now withdrawing his forces from the Rapidan. Soon after, Buford received the original orders to not cross to the south side of the Rapidan—orders that arrived nearly a day late.

**"Afton" was the home of Samuel Bradford, whose sister, Louisa Bradford, married Horatio Wright in 1842. At the time of the Bristoe campaign, Maj. Gen. Wright led a division in the Army of the Potomac's VI Corps.** (cm)

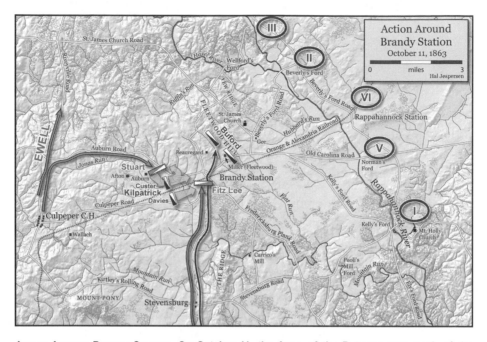

**ACTION AROUND BRANDY STATION**—On October 11, the Army of the Potomac was north of the Rappahannock River. Lee pondered his next move after Meade eluded the trap Lee had tried to spring on him. Lee decided to attempt another flanking maneuver around Meade's western flank, with his destination being Warrenton. Meanwhile, a Federal cavalry division under Brig. Gen. John Buford was still near the Rapidan River and began a quick fighting withdraw northward to rejoin the rest of the army. Maj. Gen. Jeb Stuart saw an opportunity to cut off the Federal cavalry divisions of Brig. Gen. Judson Kilpatrick (near Culpeper) and Buford (near Stevensburg) from the rest of the Army of the Potomac, setting up a severe clash of cavalry around Brandy Station.

Buford began plans to get his division back across the Rapidan. He immediately took possession of abandoned Confederate earthworks and started crossing his cavalry at Morton's Ford to the northern bank of the river. As Chapman's brigade was crossing, though, Confederate cavalry under Lomax appeared and began skirmishing with Devin. Then the crossing ran into a snag: the ford had to be "repaired" for wheeled traffic to get across safely. This took enough time that Devin soon faced both Lomax and Chambliss's brigades of cavalry.

Devin held them off, and by the time the Confederates began an all-out press against the ford, most of the brigade was across. Federal artillery deployed on the northern bank covered Devin's rear guard. Soon, all of Buford's division was across—but the threat was not over.

Just west of Morton's Ford is Raccoon Ford, another well-suited crossing over the Rapidan. Fitz

Lee planned to take Owen's brigade and the small brigade of infantry under Garrett across Raccoon Ford and trap Buford between his force and the brigades of Chambliss and Lomax. Buford was not naive to the Raccoon Ford crossing, though, and moved Chapman's brigade west to set up a defensive position near the Stringfellow farm. As the Confederates moved eastward to meet them, they noticed an apparently unsupported Federal battery. Fitz Lee ordered Owen to charge it and then push on to Morton's Ford.

Unfortunately for Owen, the battery was well supported.

Leading the 1st Virginia and 3rd Virginia in a charge against the dismounted Federal troopers, Owen realized his predicament and extracted his men from the danger. After a sharp back-and-forth action, Garrett's infantry arrived and forced Federals to fall back. This action allowed Buford to complete his crossing, though, and he moved north towards Stevensburg.

Fitz Lee's cavalry remained in pursuit.

Federal Maj. Gen. John Buford was at his peak during the Bristoe campaign. One of the most accomplished Federal cavalry commanders, Buford would only have a few months left to live, succumbing to typhoid in December. (loc)

*    *    *

Jeb Stuart, meanwhile, continued effectively screening Lee's infantry from Federal cavalry as the butternut foot soldiers marched northeast from Madison. What Stuart could not account for, though, were the various signal stations that still existed around Culpeper. They could all clearly see the Confederate movement.

In response, Meade issued orders at 4 p.m. to move the Army of the Potomac northward over the Rappahannock River to safety.

The Federal quartermasters were efficient in their retreat. Nothing was left behind for the Confederates to seize. Meade's men were "removing or destroying stores" in and around Culpeper.

Kilpatrick screened the movement and planned to link up with Buford who was now moving northward from Morton's Ford in a running battle with Fitz Lee's cavalry.

By 2 a.m. Meade's infantry began crossing bridges laid across the Rappahannock. Meade wired Halleck on the morning of October 11 that "the enemy are either moving to my right and rear or moving down on my flank, I cannot tell which, as their movements are not developed." He was prepared to meet either threat. The news of Meade's indecision on Lee's whereabouts did not sit well with the administration in Washington. "Attack him and you will soon find out," Halleck advised Meade.

Maj. Gen. Fitzhugh Lee was one of Stuart's most trusted and reliable cavalry commanders. Though aggressive, he was not able to destroy Buford's division before it crossed to the north side of the Rapidan River. (loc)

**This sketch of the Confederate defenses at Morton's Ford was drawn by Federal engineers in 1863. The hills above Morton's Ford made a significant defensive position for the Confederates from 1862-1864.** (gnmp)

As Lee's infantry awoke on the morning of October 11 near Slate Mills and Boston (VA), the Federal army was well on its way north to the Rappahannock.

Stuart moved forward through Culpeper and engaged Kilpatrick's cavalry, who were acting as the rearguard of the Army of the Potomac. Kilpatrick pulled back along the Orange & Alexandria Railroad to the east of Culpeper even as Stuart searched for a way to cut him off from the rest of Meade's army.

As Stuart looked for a way to get around Kilpatrick, Fitz Lee's fighting pursuit of Buford's cavalry continued northward from Morton's Ford toward Stevensburg. There, he was forced to make a stand. Off in the distance, he could see a Federal supply train moving north; if he didn't stand, the supply train would surely be captured.

Fitz Lee ordered Owen to lead his brigade forward and dislodge the Federals. Buford was able to repulse the Southerners' successive attacks on his flanks, disengaging as Lee's remaining cavalry arrived. Though the Confederates claimed victory at Stevensburg, the main reason for Buford's withdraw was that the supply train he was protecting cleared the Rappahannock. Also, Buford was still deep in enemy territory. As he moved north from Stevensburg to Brandy Station, Buford still wondered where the rest of the Federal cavalry and infantry were located. "My supports are not to be found," he reported.

\*    \*    \*

As the cavalry sparred east of Culpeper, Lee's men encamped in the early afternoon northwest of the town after only a few miles of marching. Lee hadn't driven his men because he was still trying to decide what to do next.

Though freeing Culpeper had not been the objective

of his campaign, Lee entered the town as a hero. Legend has it that an older woman chided some of the younger women for fraternizing with Maj. Gen. John Sedgwick's officers during the Federal occupation. To this Lee said, "Young ladies, if the music is good, go and hear it as often as you can, and enjoy yourselves. You will find that General Sedgwick will have none but agreeable gentlemen about him."

**Many of the Federal dead from the fighting in central Virginia are buried in Culpeper's National Cemetery.** (ro)

Lee began to evaluate the situation. His goal of gaining Meade's rear or flank had failed. Furthermore, Meade was efficient in his retreat and gave Lee no opportunity to take a stab at his marching columns. Lee now had three options opened to him—but his audacity dictated that only one was acceptable.

He could remain in Culpeper and set up winter encampments, but this gained him nothing strategic and the line south of the Rapidan was more defensible than the line south of the Rappahannock. Plus, the land around Culpeper provided no forage or supplies for his army.

Second, Lee could pull back across the Rapidan and prepare for winter. Though he failed to gain an advantage on Meade, he lost nothing for the effort and had pushed Meade northward.

Finally, he could possibly conduct another flank march to try again to get behind Meade or force Meade to move out of his lines along the Rappahannock. Such a move could give Lee an opportunity to strike. Most importantly, Lee kept the initiative—something he believed was essential to a potential victory for the Confederates.

While in Culpeper, Lee noted two issues that he and his army were dealing with. One was his ill-equipped

Culpeper, founded in 1759, was caught in between two large armies in September-October 1863. The central Virginia town hosted both armies throughout the war. Poet Walt Whitman, on a visit to Culpeper, wrote it "must be one of the pleasantest towns in Virginia." (loc)

supply line. The wagons were woefully inadequate, and the long route they took forced Lee's infantry to march slower than he wished. The campaign depended on quick movement, and to do that the men required constant supply. Lee constantly reminded Brig. Gen. Alexander Lawton, the newly appointed quartermaster, that the success of his campaign depended on the supply of his army.

Lee's men felt the pinch. "We did not get into camp til after dark . . ." wrote James Graham of the 27th North Carolina, "and our wagons did not come up and most of us were left without anything to eat next morning."

Another issue Lee dealt with was the leaking of information to the Richmond press. Lee wrote to Davis on October 11 that he "regretted to hear that it was announced in one of the Richmond papers of yesterday that this army was in motion and had crossed the Rapidan." He might not be able to control the Federal spies and signal towers, but he felt the Confederate government could control what the Richmond press was reporting. Lee knew his campaign depended on speed and some sort of secrecy, and he wasn't getting either.

\*    \*    \*

As Lee prepared for his next move, Stuart moved his cavalry division northward from Culpeper, using the road from Chestnut Fork Church to Fleetwood Hill in an attempt to reach the heights before Kilpatrick's cavalry. As Stuart's men got in the vicinity of the

Bradford home of Afton, they could see Kilpatrick's horsemen racing along the Orange & Alexandria Railroad towards Brandy Station. Also, Stuart could hear firing in the far distance towards Stevensburg.

With Fitz Lee pushing Buford northward and with Stuart chasing Kilpatrick, the Confederates had an opportunity to possibly destroy the two divisions of Federal cavalry isolated south of the Rappahannock.

Stuart had with him nearly 1,500 troopers in

View of Fleetwood Hill from the south. Buford was successful in reaching the vital heights before Stuart could cut him off. Securing the heights allowed the Federal cavalry to safely cross the Rappahannock River. (pr)

View from Fleetwood Hill looking towards the village of Brandy Station and Mount Pony. In 2015, the Civil War Trust completed a major purchase to preserve the historic hill. (pr)

Home of notable unionist John Minor Botts, "Auburn" played host to almost every general in the Army of the Potomac and Army of Northern Virginia during the war. It was here that Confederate cavalry launched an attack at Kilpatrick's cavalry column at Brandy Station on October 11. The privately owned home still stands today. (loc)

two brigades under Gordon and Young, while Kilpatrick could boast nearly 5,000 troopers under Brig. Gen. George A. Custer and Brig. Gen. Henry Davies. Supporting Kilpatrick was the artillery of Lt. Alexander Pennington's Battery M, 2nd U.S. Artillery. Also riding with Kilpatrick that day was Federal cavalry commander Maj. Gen. Alfred Pleasonton.

Both sides sought to secure vital heights called Fleetwood Hill, an area well known to both sides from their battle there in June. There, the Federals could easily defend against attacks until they could cross to the north side of the Rappahannock and join the infantry. If the Confederates gained the heights, though, they could possibly block Kilpatrick and Buford from the infantry and potentially destroy both divisions. Kilpatrick's men had the more direct route via the railroad, but needed to deal with both Stuart and Fitz Lee on his flanks.

Seeing the Federal cavalry in column, Stuart ordered the 1st North Carolina to harass Kilpatrick's rearguard, which consisted of the 7th Michigan and Pennington's artillery. Firing by section and then retiring, the artillery was soon overrun and temporarily captured by the Tar Heels. Severely pressed, the 7th Michigan fought off the North Carolinians repeatedly. The Carolinians were tasked to harass the Federal column to allow Stuart to get in front. Their constant

attacks successfully slowed Kilpatrick's movement to Fleetwood Hill.

Leading Stuart's column, the 12th Virginia charged across the fields of Auburn and momentarily cut through the Federal cavalry. This blocked the road to Brandy Station, which the 18th Pennsylvania was ordered to reopen. The two units struggled bitterly, with Stuart calling for the rest of his regiments to support the Virginians.

That support was the 4th and 5th North Carolina. The Tar Heels formed in column in a sunken roadbed and prepared to assist the Virginians, but before they moved forward, the undermanned 2nd New York caught them off guard and attacked their right flank. Partially trapped in the roadbed, the North Carolinians dispersed. Soon the 7th Virginia, which was delayed by taking the wrong road, attacked the now-disorganized 2nd New York and threw them back towards the railroad.

Stuart soon found himself without more men to throw into the attack and slow Kilpatrick. Fitz Lee's men neared Brandy Station, and his artillery began firing into Buford's men, as well as friendly fire into Stuart's horsemen. Though they fought hard, the Confederates under Stuart could not stop Kilpatrick's larger force from reaching Fleetwood Heights.

Soon Fitz Lee's troopers were on the scene, though somewhat unaware of Kilpatrick's position. Lomax had ordered the 15th Virginia to ride to Brandy Station and capture some apparently unattended wagons. As

At the time of the war, Brandy Station was a small rail village. During the war, both sides used it as a supply depot at various times. (loc)

**Maj. Gen. Alfred Pleasonton (standing, center) was widely known as a self-promoter and average commander of cavalry. He frequently went behind his superiors' backs to pull political strings to accomplish his goals. During the Bristoe campaign, he attached himself to Kilpatrick's division. (loc)**

the 15th Virginia moved up the Orange & Alexandria railroad, Davies ordered the 1st Vermont to clear the tracks. Seeing the 1st Vermont and the rest of Federal brigades, Maj. Charles Collins of the 15th Virginia wisely ordered his men to withdraw.

Unfortunately for the Confederates, the various attacks of the 2nd New York and 18th Pennsylvania allowed Buford to clear Fitz Lee and gain Fleetwood Hill. Kilpatrick's men were still in danger of being cut off, though, and Brig. Gen. Thomas Rosser—part of Fitz Lee's cavalry—decided to interpose his brigade between Kilpatrick and Buford. As soon as the 5th and 6th Virginia of Rosser's brigade set up near Brandy Station, a large Federal brigade came charging out of nearby woods. This was the 1st and 5th Michigan, personally led by Custer. With his band playing "Yankee Doodle," Custer's brash attack shocked and scattered the Virginians. With Custer in control of Brandy Station, the road to Fleetwood was clear for the rest of Kilpatrick's division.

Soon Buford and Kilpatrick's divisions were united atop Fleetwood Hill, with Stuart and Fitz Lee in Brandy Station. Bloody but inconclusive charge-and-countercharge then took place over the open fields around the heights. "The scene had become wild and exciting," wrote Col. Edward Sawyer of the 1st Vermont.

Stuart saw the folly in the attacks and attempted to find a way around the Federals on the hill. A lull in battle, though, allowed the Federal cavalry to successfully leave the field and safely cross to the north of the Rappahannock.

Losses are hard to determine as most reports combined all casualties from the entire campaign. But looking at unit losses and where they were engaged, the Confederates suffered at least 76 casualties and the Federals suffered nearly 280 casualties—the majority of those were reported captured or missing.

The opportunity to cut off two divisions of Federal cavalry had passed, but Stuart accomplished his mission of screening Lee's infantry and keeping Meade in the dark about Lee's intentions. Kilpatrick, too, was successful in covering Meade's withdrawal, and Buford safely escaped his situation south of the Rapidan.

Meanwhile, as Lee planned on his next flanking maneuver, Meade was planning on a bold offensive.

## At Culpeper and Brandy Station

Culpeper County was one of the most fought-over counties in Virginia during the Civil War. Its geographic location between the Rappahannock and Rapidan rivers, as well as the path of the Orange & Alexandria Railroad, made Culpeper an area desolated by the marching armies. Though suburban sprawl has begun to take hold, local preservationists and organizations have worked hard to preserve legacies of Culpeper's Civil War past.

Begin your visit at the Museum of Culpeper History located in the historic train station at 113 South Commerce St. The museum has a significant focus on the Civil War. Nearby at the northwest corner of Main and Davis Streets is the boyhood home of A. P. Hill. Finally, the National Cemetery located at 306 U.S. Avenue was established in 1866. It contains the remains of Federal dead from various battles across central Virginia.

West of town on Evans St./Sperryville Pike (Rt. 522) is Fairview Cemetery. It was here on these heights that Confederate cavalry pushed out the remaining Federal cavalry from Culpeper Courthouse on October 11, 1863. Also a few miles west on Sperryville Pike is Stonehouse Mountain and Griffinsburg, the Confederate bivouac site on October 11.

The next stop is Fleetwood Hill on the Brandy Station battlefield. From downtown Culpeper, take

Main St/Rt. 229 northward approximately two miles and make a right on Chestnut Fork Rd. At the end of Chestnut Fork Rd. take a right onto Auburn Rd. This will lead you to Brandy Station. You will be driving along the same route that Stuart's cavalry took to cut off the Federal retreat from Culpeper. The Federal cavalry under Kilpatrick rode along the railroad while Stuart took side roads. The goal was the village of Brandy Station and Fleetwood Hill beyond.

As you drive along Auburn Rd., you will pass by Afton and Auburn, two homes that stood during the war. Afton was owned by Samuel Bradford, whose daughter married Federal Maj. Gen. Horatio Wright before the war. The house can be seen from Bradford Rd. Auburn can be seen on the right of Auburn Rd. about two miles past the intersection with Inlet Road. Auburn was the home of John Botts, a famous Virginia Unionist. The home was used many times by both sides as a headquarters. Both locations are private property. It was in this vicinity that Stuart saw Federal cavalry under Kilpatrick racing along the railroad to your right. Stuart also could hear Lee and Buford battling near Stevensburg to the south.

Continue on to Fleetwood Hill at 20398 Fleetwood Heights Rd. This property was preserved in 2014 by the Civil War Trust and is a perfect location to see the landscape of the area. Facing the highway, the Rappahannock River will be behind you and the village of Brandy Station in front of you. The trail here focuses on the June 9, 1863, battle of Brandy Station, but it was here on October 11, 1863, that Buford was able to set up a defensive line to protect the retreat route for the Federal cavalry.

Finally nearby is the Graffiti House located at 19484 Brandy Rd. The house is open seasonally for tours that cover the June 9 battle of Brandy Station and the preserved soldier graffiti on the walls inside.

## ➡ To Stop 4

*Continue on Fleetwood Heights Road and make a right onto Beverly Ford Road and then your immediate left onto Route 29 north. Drive 16 miles north on Route 29 and take Meetze Road (Route 643) west towards downtown Warrenton. At the end of Meetze Road, take a right onto Falmouth St./Main St. This will take you through historic downtown Warrenton with many remaining war time structures. The Fauquier History*

Museum at the Old Jail is located on the left next to the courthouse. If you wanted to follow the general route of Ewell's infantry column to Warrenton, take Rt. 229 north from Culpeper and make a right onto Springs Road. This road will take you through Jeffersonton and to Warrenton. A. P. Hill's infantry marched farther west through Amissville and Waterloo and entered Warrenton on modern day Rt. 211.

GPS: N 38.713699, W 77.795914

Culpeper's most notable Confederate was Lt. Gen. A. P. Hill. Hill's family owned many farms and buildings in town. Hill's boyhood home still stands at the corner of Davis and Main Streets. (cm)

# "Lee is Unquestionably Bullying You"

## CHAPTER FOUR
### Oct. 11-13, 1863

As night fell across Brandy Station on October 11, Lee settled on his next move. His aggressive nature led him toward another flanking maneuver around Meade's western flank. He ordered a portion of Stuart's cavalry to screen the march, with Col. Oliver Funsten's brigade of cavalry leading Ewell's infantry to Sulphur Springs, a popular crossing on the Rappahannock north of the Federal infantry that had concentrated at Rappahannock Station. Lee also ordered Young's cavalry brigade to take position in Culpeper to protect the supply base Lee was now creating for his move to Warrenton. Detaching a significant cavalry force in the Culpeper-Brandy Station area would have unintended consequences and keep Meade guessing on the Confederate intentions.

While Ewell and the cavalry were moving on a narrow arc from Culpeper to Sulphur Spring, A. P. Hill's corps again took the wider arc and began to move towards the village of Amissville. It was here in August 1862 that "Stonewall" Jackson began his wide flanking maneuver around Pope that led to the battle of Second Manassas. Many of the men in Hill's corps remembered that feat, as William Long of the 44th North Carolina wrote, "If Old Stonewall was here we'd get him sure."

The Army of the Potomac was now strung out on the north bank of the Rappahannock River. Brig Gen. D. M. Gregg's cavalry division covered the western flank around Sulphur Springs and was on the lookout for any Confederates marching farther west. Gregg sent out the 1st Maine cavalry on a reconnaissance to Sperryville, located along the foothills of the Blue Ridge. These cavalrymen ended up on an adventure that lasted nearly 48 hours as

The Rogues Road climbs from Auburn to around Coffee Hill. On October 13, the Federal III Corps took this road to Greenwich. On the morning of October 14, Brig. Gen. Caldwell's men were on the right side of the road. (ro)

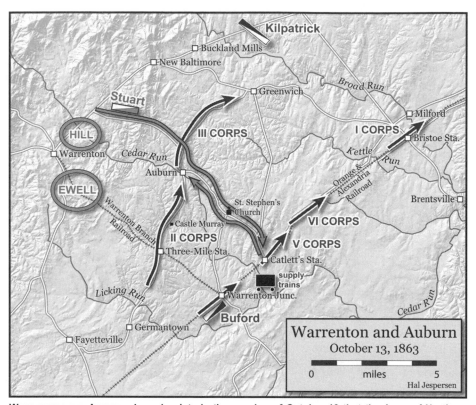

**Warrenton and Auburn**—Learning late in the evening of October 12 that the Army of Northern Virginia was near Warrenton and his army was partially south of the Rappahannock River, Maj. Gen. George Meade ordered a night march northward to Centreville. Midday on October 13, the two wings of the Army of Northern Virginia reunited in Warrenton. Holding the initiative and sitting on Meade's flank, Lee had the opportunity to push on and get behind the Army of the Potomac—but a broken-down supply system forced him to go into bivouac so his army could resupply. Meanwhile, Maj. Gen. Jeb Stuart led a scouting mission towards Catlett Station to locate the Army of the Potomac. On his return westward, Stuart found himself between the marching columns of Meade's army and hid out the evening of October 13, calling on Lee for help.

they became stuck behind Confederate lines (covered in Appendix A).

Meade, too, was weighing his options. With an ever-constant interest in the army's movements by his superiors in Washington, Meade was sensitive to the fact that his army had pulled back. Halleck reminded Meade that Lee was minus Longstreet and that some reports from Chattanooga stated that Ewell was out west (this was, of course, inaccurate). In a blunt message, Halleck wrote to Meade: "Lee is unquestionably bullying you."

Like many generals before him, Meade began overestimating Lee's numbers. Even with Longstreet's corps gone, Meade continued to predict Lee had nearly 80,000 men—nearly equal to his own numbers.

In reality, Lee could only claim 53,000 men in his ranks compared to Meade's 89,000. Halleck stated to Meade that Lee could have no more than "40,000 or 45,000 infantry and over 5,000 cavalry"—a very accurate assessment.

Ever present-minded that he could easily be removed from command, Meade began to take an aggressive tone. He was unsure of Lee's intentions and received no word of Confederate infantry on his right. He also continued to get reports that the Confederates were still in force around Culpeper. In a bold move, he decided to re-cross to the south side of the Rappahannock. "If Lee will give me battle between the Rappahannock and the Rapidan," Meade wrote, "I will fight him."

The move, ordered at 10:30 a.m., would involve the V Corps, VI Corps, and Buford's cavalry, all placed under the command of Maj. General Sedgwick. The mission was to seek out Lee and, if he was in place at Culpeper, offer battle. Facing them would be elements of Young's cavalry brigade screening Culpeper, and Rosser's cavalry brigade screening the Confederate infantry's flanking maneuver.

At the same time Meade was about to launch his offensive, Gregg's cavalry—in the area of

Founded in 1798 and named in honor of Thomas Jefferson, Jeffersonton was a modest village in 1863. The cemetery of the rebuilt Jeffersonton Baptist Church contains Confederate graves from battles in this area in 1862 and 1863. (ro)

A hard-fighting cavalry commander, Brig. Gen. David Gregg commanded the far western flank of the Army of the Potomac on October 12. His delaying tactics held up Lee at Jeffersonton and, later that evening, he informed Meade of the danger of being flanked. After the campaign, Gregg took issue with Meade for not commending his command in the official report. (loc)

One of Meade's most trusted commanders, Maj. Gen. John Sedgwick, was given command of the mobile force that moved back across the Rappahannock in search of Lee. (loc)

Sulphur Springs and Jeffersonton—began to skirmish with Confederate cavalry under Funsten. These Confederates were the lead elements of Ewell's column attempting to cross the Rappahannock at Sulphur Springs. After a sharp fight, Gregg's forward regiment, the 13th Pennsylvania Cavalry, pulled back to the Rappahannock River. Soon more of Gregg's division came to their support and pushed the Confederates back out of Jeffersonton.

Now Stuart was on the scene and so were the leading elements of Ewell's infantry.

Stuart saw an opportunity to cut off the Federal cavalry in Jeffersonton from the crossing at Sulphur Springs. He ordered infantry to confront the Federals head on while Confederate cavalry attempted to flank and get around the Federal rear. Soon Confederates began to fire into the rear of the Federal cavalry in the village. The realization that their route to the river was closed created panic in the Federal horsemen. A few stood their ground, such as Pvt. Michael Dougherty of the 13th Pennsylvania, who was awarded the Medal of Honor for being at the head of his detachment in a charge and leading a staunch defense in the village.

Most of the Federals, though, broke into a panic and fled back to the Rappahannock. The Confederates captured several hundred prisoners and horses. Gregg decided to consolidate his remaining men at Sulphur Springs and attempt to thwart the Confederate crossing. He posted his dismounted cavalry on hills above the bridge in old rifle pits, then unlimbered Battery A, 4th U.S. Artillery, above the crossing. Gregg also ordered the bridge planks removed.

By 2 p.m., Stuart was ready to attack Gregg at Sulphur Springs. Stuart sent the 7th and 11th Virginia north to another ford to outflank the Federals. The 12th Virginia attacked directly and tried to cross the bridge with the support of Lt. Col. Thomas Carter's artillery battalion from Ewell's corps. The Confederate artillery quickly forced the single Federal battery from the crossing even as the 12th Virginia—realizing the bridge planks were missing—splashed across the river up to the other side.

Fighting swirled around the Fauquier White Sulphur Springs resort, just north of the bridge. A battalion of Confederate sharpshooters entered the resort, firing on the Federal cavalry from the resort buildings. Tired and still recovering from the ordeal in Jeffersonton, by sunset the Federal resistance began to break. Outnumbered, Gregg

pulled southeastward to Fayetteville, uncovering the road to Warrenton.

Gregg suffered nearly 10 percent casualties among his whole division, with the majority being captured. Lee, present for the fighting, crossed the repaired bridge at Sulphur Springs with the lead elements of Ewell's infantry. Lee's health had improved, and now he was riding Traveler, not in an ambulance.

Confederates were now on the flank of and behind Meade's Army of the Potomac. Though Gregg forwarded a message to Pleasonton—who was with Meade—at 4:50 p.m., for unknown reasons, the message of the action and the Confederate presence in Meade's rear and flank did not reach headquarters until later that evening.

In the meantime, Meade nervously waited for some word from Gregg about any inclination that Lee was moving around his right. Not finding Lee in force near Brandy Station, Meade became more worried about unsubstantiated—and untrue—reports that Confederates were seen near Manassas Gap. "Lee may get between me and Washington," Meade wired Washington, "and you may be annoyed then."

Reading these words, Halleck and Lincoln must have been shocked. Just three months earlier, both had believed Meade should have destroyed Lee after Gettysburg; now that battle seemed for naught.

The county seat of Fauquier County, Warrenton spent most of the war occupied by Federal forces. One Federal cavalryman observed that "great distress prevails among the citizens hereabouts for the necessities of life." (loc)

**A rare wartime photograph of the Fauquier White Sulphur Springs hotel shows the toll of four years of war on the once-luxurious hotel, which was eventually destroyed.** (loc)

Around 9 p.m., Gregg's report finally reached Meade. Now Meade knew that Lee's army was positioned on his western flank. Immediately Meade began to lay out marching orders to all his commanders for a night march northward — a difficult task. Lee was obviously either trying to get behind him or strike his flank. Either way, being on the south side of the Rappahannock with Lee on the north side was not a good place to be. Timing was now of the essence.

The Gray Fox had again stolen a march — but this time, the Army of the Potomac's commander was up to the task.

\* \* \*

As Meade decided to move northward, Lee's infantry bivouacked for the night. Ewell's men, after their small battle at Sulphur Springs, camped around the once-luxurious resort. This put them eight miles south of Warrenton. A. P. Hill's men had a less-adventurous day; leaving the area around Griffinsburg, they marched north and crossed the Hazel River near Hill's Mill (owned by A. P.'s brother, Thomas). They moved north from there and bivouacked around the village of Amissville, 12 miles west of Warrenton. Though Hill's men were not north of the Rappahannock yet, Ewell's corps was—and in a great position to cause Meade much trouble the next day.

Lee's plan for October 13 was to continue

Home of the widow of Judge John Tyler, the house played host to a dinner in honor of Gen. Robert E. Lee and Lt. Gen. Richard Ewell on October 13. (fcpl)

to march northward to gain Meade's western flank or possibly his rear and route of supply and communication. Ewell would march from Sulphur Springs to Warrenton and link up with Hill's corps there. Then, within supporting distance of each other, they would continue northward.

At 9:00 a.m., the head of Ewell's column arrived in Warrenton after only marching eight miles. The Confederate supply trains were still woefully slow, and the men needed to draw rations. Ewell's corps went into camp around noon about a mile east of town near the Rock Hill Road.

By early afternoon, Hill's corps arrived in Warrenton via the Waterloo Road and began drawing rations from the slowly arriving supply trains. This proved to be a strategic mishap on Lee's part. By mid-day on the 13th, Lee was in a good position to either attack Meade's flank or march his army around to Meade's rear. Unlike the days of 1862, however—when the Confederate army marched swiftly through the area to gain the rear of the Federal army under Maj. Gen. John Pope—Lee allowed the Army of Northern Virginia to go into camp with plenty of daylight left. The nagging problems of his Quartermaster and Subsistence Departments began to take a toll on Lee's effectiveness in the field.

Meade, meanwhile, continued his forced march northward along the line of the Orange & Alexandria Railroad.

**The modern St. Stephen's Church stands in the historic location of the wartime church. It was here that Stuart left his cavalry as he scouted out towards Catlett Station on October 13.** (pr)

Around 10 a.m., Lee ordered Stuart to take his cavalry and ride east to find the Army of the Potomac and report on their location and line of march and scout out other details that could be helpful in Lee's plans. Stuart took his own division and Brig. Gen. Lunsford Lomax's brigade with him towards Catlett. After clearing the important crossroads of Auburn, Stuart left Lomax behind to protect the crossroads and maintain communication with Warrenton.

Stuart arrived on the hills above Catlett later that morning, and what Stuart saw before him must have brought a smile to his face. Parked in and around the fields of Catlett was the majority of the Army of the Potomac's supply train, with thousands of wagons and teamsters all ignorant to the threat of the Confederate cavalry. Buford's Federal cavalry division was also nearby—and also unaware of Stuart.

More importantly, Stuart had located the bulk of Meade's army and realized that the Confederates were in a great position that day to strike Meade. With the Confederate infantry only nine miles away, the timing was perfect. "I believe you can reach the rear if Hill is up," Stuart messaged Lee.

But soon Stuart's joy turned to concern as he

received word of large Federal infantry in his rear. Lomax's men, guarding the important crossroads, found themselves confronted with the entire III Corps under Maj. General French. Amazingly, French himself with his staff led the column with no scouts in front. The Confederate cavalrymen opened fire, and a bullet went through French's hat. "Had it gone through his heart or head," wrote Pvt. John Haley of the 17th Maine, "it would not have grieved us."

The III Corps quickly brought its strength to bear, pushing Lomax out of Auburn. Worsening matters, the II Corps appeared in the area, as well.

Stuart was cut off from Lee.

\* \* \*

The Federals that Lomax and Stuart encountered were part of Meade's retrograde plan to guard his western flank. Once he learned of Confederate infantry on his western flank, Meade had his men march directly for Centreville, ordering the III and II corps to march north following the path of the old Rogues Road from Fayettville to Auburn and Greenwich. These two corps would be in supporting distance of each other and would screen the rest of the Army of the Potomac, which marched north along the Orange & Alexandria Railroad from Rappahannock Station.

New research suggests this location as the position of Stuart and his cavalry on the evening of October 13. This narrow valley was only a few hundred yards from encamped Federals. (cm)

Warren, leading the II Corps, grew weary of French's inability to keep up a timely march. Understanding the need for a quick march because of the danger they were in, Warren fretted as French seemed to take his time. Warren wanted to clear the crossroads of Auburn and ford Cedar Run by the night of the 13th, but French's tardiness meant he would have to cross the next morning. Worse yet, French did not stay in supporting distance and was bivouacking his corps several miles northward near Greenwich. The II Corps would be on its own this night.

Also on his own that night was Jeb Stuart. Leaving

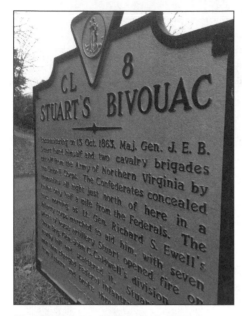

The Virginia state historic marker suggests one of the possible locations of Stuart's hideout on the evening of October 13. (cm)

Brig. Gen. Lunsford Lomax's Virginia cavalry brigade was left in Auburn on October 13 to protect Stuart's rear. Heavily outnumbered, Lomax was forced to surrender the crossroads to the Federal III Corps. Lomax had a mixed record for the rest of the war. He died in Washington, D.C., in 1913 and is buried in the Warrenton Cemetery. (loc)

Catlett, he rode back to find Auburn in Federal hands. Lomax was no match for two Federal corps, and he rode west to join with Fitz Lee's cavalry. Stuart considered his options: Riding east was not possible because there were at least 20,000 Federals in that direction. Riding north was out of the question as the III Corps blocked that route. He could not ride south or west as the II Corps blocked his routes that way.

Stuart decided to "conceal my whereabouts, if possible, from the enemy" and hide his two brigades of cavalry in a small ravine a few hundred yards east of Auburn. Surrounded by low-lying hills with a small creek running along the floor of the ravine, the area was narrow near the road but broadened northward from the road. A small patch of woods along the road concealed the entrance, and it could fit Stuart's two brigades, wagons, and horse artillery. Nearly a thousand horses, mules, and men hid in the small ravine as thousands of Federals marched and camped within 150 yards.

Those who experienced it remembered well that night—one of the tensest nights of the war for the Confederate cavalry. "We were so close to the enemy," recalled W. W. Blackford, "that it was necessary to place a man at the head of every mule in the ambulances to keep them from betraying our presence."

"The men sat motionless and silent in the saddle, listening, throughout the long hours of the night," wrote John Esten Cooke after the war. "No man spoke, no sound was heard from human lips." Henry McClellan summed up the thoughts of many of the Confederates that night: "How thankful we were for those hills! How thankful for that darkness!"

Stuart decided to send five riders to alert Lee, hoping at least one would get through the Federal lines. These men would have to navigate through Federal infantry and cavalry pickets then ride hard for Warrenton, six miles to the west. Stuart wrote later that he believed a great opportunity could arise if he could "cooperate with any attack made by our main body upon the flank." But this was hindsight for Stuart; on the night of the 13th he was mostly concerned with escape.

That same night, II Corps commander G. K. Warren slept uneasy at the home of Col. Edward Murray, a prewar army friend. Warren knew that Confederate cavalry was present in the area. He also knew that Lee and his infantry were not far away to his west. If Lee were to attack, it would be his II Corps that bore the brunt. He had no confidence that he would receive support from French.

Warren's fears would soon become reality.

"Castle Murray" was built by Dr. James Murray and called "Melrose" during the war. It has been mislabeled by most as Maj. Gen. G. K. Warren's headquarters on October 13. Warren's headquarters was actually at "Rock Hill," the nearby home of prewar friend Col. Edward Murray. (loc)

## At Warrenton

Any visit to Warrenton should start at the Fauquier History Museum at the Old Jail. Located at 10 Ashby St. in Warrenton, exhibits cover the entire history of the area, but with a specific concentration on the Civil War. In front of the museum is a monument to Col. John S. Mosby as well as the first stop on the Bristoe Station Campaign Mobile Tour, developed by Prince William County and Fauquier County. Located just west of the museum is the Warrenton Cemetery. Many notables are buried here, including Col.

Today the location of the Tyler house is a modern strip of stores in downtown Warrenton. Many other Civil War-era buildings in Warrenton still stand. (ro)

John Mosby and nearly 600 Confederates from all over the south.

To the west on Waterloo Street/Road is where A. P. Hill's men marched into Warrenton from Amissville. Near the intersection Waterloo Road and Broadview Avenue (Business Rt. 17 and 211) is the location of Hill's bivouac.

Further west, the historic location of Waterloo Bridge still exists. The current bridge is a postwar structure, but on the same location as the wartime bridge. The bridge was used by Hill to cross Rappahannock before moving east to Warrenton. Ewell's men arrived from Sulphur Springs on modern day Culpeper St. (Springs Road). His corps bivouacked southeast of town near the intersection of Falmouth St. and Old Meetze Road. Sandie Pendleton wrote that Ewell (and presumably Lee) enjoyed dinner at the home of Mrs. Tyler on the evening of October 13. Mrs. Tyler was the widow of Judge John Webb Tyler, a distant relative of Ewell's. The home no longer stands but was located on Main St., between 4th and 5th Street, across the street from the Warrenton Presbyterian Church.

To reach Sulphur Springs, the scene of the cavalry battle between Stuart and Gregg, take Culpeper St. south and follow Springs Road. This will lead you to the Fauquier Springs Country Club, the modern location of the Fauquier White Sulphur Springs Resort, where a few war time buildings survive today. To reach Jeffersonton, continue on Springs Road, crossing the Rappahannock River and in three miles the Jeffersonton Baptist Church will be on your left. The church was rebuilt after the war, but it was in the center of the fighting in Jeffersonton on October 12.

# ➡ To Stop 5

*From the Old Jail Museum, take Main St. east and make a left onto Meetze Road (Rt. 643). Take Meetze Road for 5.3 miles and make a left onto Casanova Road (Rt. 616). You are now following the route of the Federal II and III corps. Stay on Casanova Road for one mile and make a left onto Weston Road (Rt. 747) and then your immediate left onto Rogues Road (Rt. 602) at the village of Casanova. Casanova is war time "Three Mile Station."*

*After 1.3 miles, Castle Murray (Melrose) will be on your right (private property). A wartime structure, it has been mistakenly labeled in many histories as Warren's headquarters. Warren actually stayed at Col. Edward Murray's house (Rock Hill), a few hundred yards south of here (no longer standing). Castle Murray was the home of Dr. James Murray.*

*Continue on for another two miles and pull over at the Auburn historic marker on the right.*

GPS: N 38.702080, W 77.701810

# The Battle of Auburn

## CHAPTER FIVE
### Oct. 14, 1863

Lee received his first report of Stuart's predicament at 4 a.m. Patiently listening to the courier, Lee then returned to his tent. The courier, frustrated that Lee didn't appreciate the urgency of Stuart's predicament, started chatting with some of Lee's staff officers. Lee overheard and pushed angrily from his tent to scold the courier for sharing sensitive information without permission. Lee's staff explained to the commander that the scout meant no harm and was assisting the staff in their ability to understand the situation. Lee calmed, then offered the courier a meal at his personal table in his tent. The stress of the campaign and Stuart's predicament was getting to the commanding general.

Lee, in fact, reacted quickly to the courier's news and ordered Ewell to relieve Stuart from his precarious position. Ewell would be on a rescue mission and not undertaking any strategic attempt to destroy the isolated II Corps. Within a few hours, Ewell's divisions were marching toward Auburn using the Rock Hill Road (modern day Meetze Road) and the Double Poplars Road.

Lee had to see how Ewell's mission developed before could he refocus on Meade. He did, however, order Hill's corps to march northward from Warrenton along the Warrenton Turnpike. This road led through the old Manassas battlefields and straight to Centreville. Hill would be called on if needed to support Ewell, but would play no major role in the action around Auburn that morning.

The 1st North Carolina cavalry charged across this field to the distant tree line, where the 126th and 125th New York waited. Some Federals formed "hallow squares" to confront the cavalry. (cm)

*    *    *

Miles away, Gouverneur K. Warren passed a mostly sleepless night at "Rock Hill," the home of his friend, Colonel Murray. Certainly, the Confederate

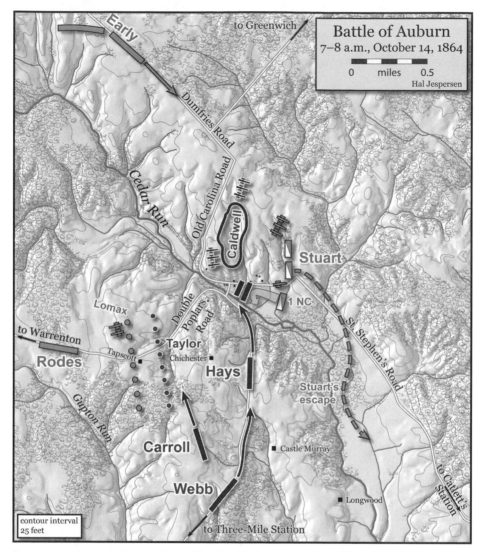

**BATTLE OF AUBURN**—On the evening of October 13, Lee received word from Maj. Gen. Jeb Stuart that his cavalry division was surrounded at Auburn. Lee ordered Lt. Gen. Richard S. Ewell to march to Stuart's rescue. On the morning of October 14, as men under Brig. Gen. John Caldwell prepared breakfast, Stuart's horse artillery began shelling the breakfasting soldiers. Soon, Ewell's infantry arrived south of Auburn, forcing Federals to react quickly to dual threats. Stuart, frustrated that Ewell's attack was not more aggressive, escaped southward along Cedar Run, thus taking Stuart out of the remainder of the campaign northward. Federals quickly moved through Auburn then eastward toward Catlett Station.

cavalry French had confronted the day before had informed Lee of the Federal presence in the area—but it would be Warren, not French, who would take any hit. Warren was the flanking force of the army, which also meant he was most in danger of being attacked by the Army of Northern Virginia. Making

him even more vulnerable, the III Corps's delays the day before had created a gap between Warren and French, who was now encamped at Greenwich five miles to the north. The rest of the Army of the Potomac was located five miles east along the Orange & Alexandria Railroad.

Meade's orders for October 14 were a continuation of his orders on the 12th and 13th: The Army of the Potomac would continue to move northward towards Centreville. To keep the corps from separating, and keep them all within supporting distance of each other, his staff identified locations along the route of march where each corps could stop and wait for the others to catch up. French and his III Corps had already failed to do so, though—thus creating the five-mile gap that left Warren vulnerable.

Just before Warren left Rock Hill, he tucked a photograph of himself in Mrs. Murray's prayer book. They had all been good friends before the war, and Warren wrote his wife later that "she is such a sweet lady; and, being all alone in the house, was much more desolate than you."

The II Corps, stretched out along the Rogues

**Dating from the 18th century, "Neavil's Mill" was an industrial center in Fauquier County. A major landmark during the battle of Auburn, the structure was restored in the 1960s as a commercial building. (ro)**

Soldiers' accounts during October 1863 vary from hot and humid to wet and cold. A typical fall in Virginia, this weather made it hard for the quartermasters to keep the men appropriately clothed. (loc)

Road, began to move before sunrise. Warren was directed to cross Cedar Run at Auburn, then march east to Catlett to join the rest of the marching army along the Orange & Alexandria Railroad. With Warren rode Gregg's cavalry division and the corps's train of 225 wagons—the focus of most of Warren's worry.

A heavy fog hung over the Cedar Run valley. "Before us lay a very picturesque valley full of farmhouses and barns," wrote Thomas Galwey of the 8th Ohio.

Auburn was located alongside the creek in a deep valley. Tall hills surrounded the village, and most were covered with patches of woods. Four roads met there, and three of them had to navigate a steep grade to reach the Cedar Run crossing, which consisted of a small bridge and treacherous ford. It made a poor position for Warren if he had to fight and a ripe place to lose his wagon train.

Brig. Gen. John Caldwell's division was the first to reach Auburn. Starting their march around 4 a.m., they took position on a "bald and tolerably prominent hill" just to the northwest of the bridge. The men and accompanying batteries of Capt. Bruce Ricketts, Capt. William Arnold, and Capt. Nelson Ames faced west—the expected approach of Lee's men. They then began to settle down to cook breakfast. The rest of the II Corps was still moving northward toward Auburn and would arrive soon.

Meanwhile, Stuart—whose location had still

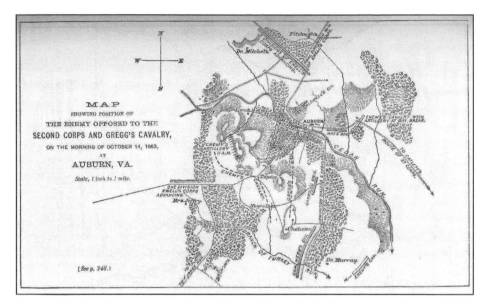

MAP

SHOWING POSITION OF

THE ENEMY OPPOSED TO THE

SECOND CORPS AND GREGG'S CAVALRY,

ON THE MORNING OF OCTOBER 14, 1863,

AT

AUBURN, VA.

Scale, 1 inch to 1 mile.

[See p. 248.]

gone unnoticed—awaited a response from the several couriers he sent out to Lee the previous night. Per his suggestions, he expected to hear the opening of a battle that would herald his rescue force from Warrenton. Stuart, ever the aggressive cavalry commander, began to see how he could make the best of his precarious situation. If Confederate infantry could press against Warren's men from the west, then he would be in a perfect position to strike their rear. They could possible destroy the Federal II Corps.

The Confederate commander in charge of rescuing Stuart was Ewell. A competent division commander, his six-month record as a corps commander was already under scrutiny. He had not shown the same aggressive spirit of his predecessor, Lt. Gen. Thomas "Stonewall" Jackson. In Ewell's defense, though, he saw this particular mission as a rescue mission, not one of coordination to possibly annihilate a corps of the Army of the Potomac. Plus, riding with Ewell was Lee, and if Lee believed aggressive action was warranted, he surely would have ordered it.

As Caldwell's division lounged along the ridge, the fog began to lift, and Stuart could see the Federals spread out over the hill in front of him. Soon firing came from the southwest where the 10th New York Cavalry began to skirmish along the Double Poplars Road with approaching Confederate cavalry under Lomax.

Gregg assisted in drawing this map of the battle of Auburn, which is included in his official report on the Bristoe campaign. (loc)

Maj. Gen. Gouverneur K. Warren's star was rising by the time of the Bristoe campaign. Considered by many a hero for "saving" Little Round Top at Gettysburg, Warren took over command of the II Corps from Maj. Gen. Winfield Hancock, who was recovering from wounds suffered at Gettysburg. (loc)

Brig. Gen. Alexander Hays, a close friend of Lt. Gen. U. S. Grant before the war, was considered a hard fighter. His personal letters to his wife during the war give great insight to the Bristoe campaign. Hays died on May 5, 1864, during the battle of the Wilderness. (loc)

Behind Lomax marched the infantry division of Maj. Gen. Robert Rodes.

As soon as Caldwell's men began to prepare for an attack from the west, artillery fire from the east erupted. Stuart, having heard the distant firing from the west, ordered Maj. Robert Beckham's seven pieces of horse artillery to move within 400 yards of Caldwell's men and open fire. Stuart hoped that with an aggressive push by Ewell's infantry, the II Corps would be pinched in a trap.

The Federals on the soon-to-be-called "Coffee Hill" were surprised and confused by the firing in their rear. As one Federal soldier wrote a few weeks later: "Congratulating ourselves that Minnie balls were harmless when we were out of range; when, quick as gunpowder, the rebels opened on us in our rear with a battery, and they planted their shells right among us. The fact of the matter is, it was decidedly bad."

However, the effect of the Confederate fire was suspect at best. As another Federal wrote, "The shells passing over our heads and exploding far away in the woods."

In response to the new threat to their rear, Caldwell's men moved to the western slope of the hill to avoid Beckham's fire. He then ordered his batteries to unlimber and return fire on the Confederate guns. Beckham was quickly outgunned and was "compelled more reluctantly to withdraw the artillery."

Soon the next II Corps division in column arrived under Brig. Gen. Alexander Hays. Hays ordered his infantry across the Cedar Run bridge towards the now-exposed Confederate cavalry position to the east. At the same time, the Confederate infantry arrived south of Auburn on the Double Poplars Road, pushing against the cavalry brigade serving as Warren's screen. Warren still had to cross Brig. Gen. Alexander Webb's division and his baggage train, so he sent Brig. Gen. Samuel Carroll's infantry brigade to assist his cavalry's defense.

The Confederates did not aggressively push their attack, though. Instead, Ewell waited for his artillery to set up. His job, he believed, was to relieve Stuart, not coordinate a major assault.

Stuart began to see that he was not going to get the infantry support he hoped for. He was outnumbered, and soon the marching II Corps would block any escape route. He needed a diversion and looked to the 1st North Carolina cavalry under Lt. Col. Thomas Ruffin.

Ruffin, a former U.S. Congressman, readily accepted the challenge. He was to take his cavalry and charge west towards the oncoming Federal infantry along the St. Stephen's Church Road. He would have support from one piece of artillery. Once Ruffin's men temporarily halted the Federal march, Stuart would take the rest of his cavalry and artillery and move eastward along the millrace north of Cedar Run.

It was a sacrificial charge to save the bulk of Stuart's cavalry.

While Ruffin prepared for his suicide mission, the 126th New York and 12th New Jersey were ordered to move east to determine the size and disposition of the Confederate force hidden there. Moving east from the area of the Auburn Mill, the New Yorkers ran smack into Ruffin and his Tar Heels.

Some of the New Yorkers formed squares, a classic defense formation against cavalry, but the horsemen began to get around the flanks of the Federals as they moved into formation, who then began to break.

The Confederate cavalrymen continued forward towards a fence on the edge of the field; there, the 12th New Jersey was hidden from sight. A sudden volley from along the fence line littered the field with dozens of wounded and dead men and horses. The charge of the 1st North Carolina was over.

One of those fallen was Ruffin himself. Wounded in several places during the charge, he lay on the ground as Federals began to recognize his rank. As men from the 12th New Jersey hovered over him, they noticed his fine gold watch. "Colonel," one of them remarked, "do please hurry up and die, we want that watch." Ruffin died shortly thereafter, and his watch was lost to history.

\*    \*    \*

With the Confederate infantry holding most of the Warren's attention, Stuart was able to take advantage of the sacrificial charge of the 1st North Carolina and move his command east and south, out of harm's way.

The II Corps was still in danger, however, with Ewell's divisions pressing on their rear and flank.

Lt. Col. Thomas Ruffin was a former U.S. Congressman from North Carolina who resigned his seat when North Carolina seceded. A member of the Confederate Provisional Congress in 1861, Ruffin joined the 1st North Carolina cavalry and had a distinguished record. (loc)

**The distant wood line is Coffee Hill from the west. Bare of any trees in 1863, here Federal troops began to prepare breakfast early in the morning on October 14. Facing west, they did not realize Confederate cavalry was less than a half-mile behind them. (cm)**

Soon, more Confederate infantry arrived—Jubal Early's division—along the Warrenton Road from the northwest in front of Coffee Hill.

Warren and his division commanders performed an excellent rearguard action to hold the Confederates at a distance, and the lack of aggressiveness by the Confederates assisted his defense. By late morning Warren was able to move his entire corps and baggage train across Cedar Run and east on the St. Stephen's Church Road to Catlett.

"To halt was to await annihilation," Warren later wrote, describing his situation.

Since Stuart was no longer in danger, Ewell's corps moved north towards Greenwich instead of following Warren east. Stuart, by moving southward to safety, took himself out of the army's advance, which would have consequences later in the day.

The II Corps would now be the rearguard of the entire Army of the Potomac and still in danger of being cut off by Lee.

As Brig. Gen. Hays wrote, "No rest for the wicked."

*At Auburn*

In front of the Auburn historic marker is Cedar Run. The current bridge is in the same location as the wartime bridge. On the road to your left is Old Auburn Road (wartime Double Poplars Road), where Fitz Lee and Ewell's infantry arrived to relieve Stuart. The location where the 10th New York and Lomax's cavalry clashed is approximately one mile up the road.

As you cross Cedar Run, in front of you is the Stephen McCormick house site. No longer standing, the building was a major landmark during the war. McCormick was an inventor of agricultural equipment and developed a revolutionary plow in 1816.

The wartime Auburn (or Neavil) Mill sits to the right. It was restored in the 1960s as a commercial building. The Miller's house sits at the left corner of the intersection. In 1863, Auburn was the home of a grist mill, a lumber mill, a tanyard, blacksmith shops, several stores and a post office.

If you take the road to the left (Rogues Road, Rt. 602), you will climb up a hill. This is the famed "Coffee Hill" where Caldwell's men were positioned. Most of the men were to the right of the road.

This important crossing created a serious logistical problem for the Federal II Corps on the early morning of October 14. Cedar Run was not fordable for wheeled traffic, and this bridge funneled the entire corps into this indefensible valley. (cm)

**This engraving from the regimental history of the 125th and 126th New York depicts the 1st North Carolina cavalry charge and the mortal wounding of Lt. Col. Thomas Ruffin. (es)**

To go to the location of Stuart's hideout and the battlefield of the 1st North Carolina, take a right after the Cedar Run bridge (Old Auburn Road, Rt. 670). In about 1/10 of a mile, you will come to a field on your right. This is where the 1st North Carolina charged the 126th New York and 12th New Jersey. The Confederate cavalry were perpendicular to the road, and the Federal infantry was near the current tree line to your right.

The location of Stuart's hideout on October 13 is still today much debated. Travel another .3 miles and the road will start to bend to the left. Look off to your left; you will see a wooded valley with a small stream. Hard to see today, this valley opens up as it moves away from the road. The authors believe this was Stuart's hidden location on the evening of October 13. If you continue on Rt. 670 and make a right onto Old Dumfries Road (Rt. 667), you will soon see a Virginia state historic marker on your right. In this vicinity is another location believed by some to be Stuart's hidden bivouac.

Please remember, all locations are on private property.

 **To Stop 6**

*From the Auburn historic marker, cross the Cedar Run bridge and make your first left onto Rogues Road (Rt. 602). You will be following in the footsteps of French's III Corps on October 13 and*

Ewell's Second Corps on October 14. At the end of Rogues Road., take a left onto Dumfries Road (Rt. 605) and then your immediate right onto Rogues Road (Rt. 602). It was near this intersection that Early's division put pressure on Caldwell from the northwest while Rodes pressured from the southwest.

At the end of Rogues Road, make a right onto Vint Hill Road (Rt. 215). Here is the village of Greenwich and the historic Greenwich Presbyterian Church (historic markers for the Bristoe Campaign and Richard Ewell's family farm are on the right side of the road in the village). Follow Vint Hill Road for six miles and take a left onto Nokesville Road (Rt. 28). The Bristow Center Shopping Center will be on your left. The best vantage point for the next stop is at the end of the Harris Teeter parking lot overlooking the pond.

If you wish to follow the route of Warren's men from Auburn to Bristoe, take a right onto Old Auburn Road (Rt. 670) after the Cedar Run bridge. Then make a right onto Old Dumfries Road (Rt. 667) and follow this road for two and a half miles. At this intersection you will see St. Stephen's Church on your left. This is the wartime location of the church. Destroyed during the war, the church was rebuilt in 1881.

Make a right onto Old Dumfries Road (Rt. 667) and take this to Catlett. It was at Catlett that Stuart observed the large Federal supply train on October 13.

Take a left onto Catlett Road (Rt. 28) and travel approximately eight miles and the Bristow Center Shopping Center is on your left.

GPS: N 38.732810, W 77.548639

# The Approach to Bristoe

## CHAPTER SIX
### Oct. 14, 1863

After a tense morning disengaging from the enemy, Warren and his II Corps made quick progress towards Catlett's Station on the Orange & Alexandria Railroad. Still, the morning's events highlighted the isolation he faced.

When the head of the column reached Catlett, instead of continuing the march, the troops received orders to halt. The rapid march from Auburn to Catlett had strung out the corps, and if it continued to march in such a fashion and was attacked, it very well could be defeated piecemeal. By halting for a few hours, Warren intended to concentrate the corps and thus be able to fend off any attacking force.

Once the rear elements of the II Corps started to stream into the small railroad stop, Warren quickly got his soldiers marching again. With the final destination being the fortifications at Centreville, Warren decided to take the most direct route, marching north along the railroad. After the surprise at Auburn, a skirmish line preceded the column to sound the alarm if any Confederate forces were located.

The march along the single-tracked railroad accelerated quickly. In order to make the march as efficient as possible, the II Corps's wagons and ambulances traveled along the many small farm roads that paralleled the railroad, while most of the infantrymen marched on the track itself. A soldier in the 1st Minnesota remembered that "a glanced backward occasionally showed a stream of swaying gun barrels and bobbing, battered, black hats surging after me, as the boys 'jumped the ties.'"

In such a formation the II Corps made good progress, with the head of the column crossing Kettle Run about two miles south of Bristoe Station around 1:30 p.m.

Built prior to the Civil War, the Presbyterian Church was the landmark of Greenwich. In October 1863, Hill's Corps marched by here on their way to Bristoe Station. (pg)

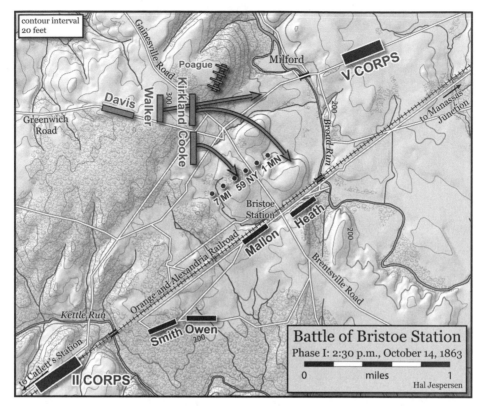

**BATTLE OF BRISTOE STATION, PHASE I**—After the battle of Auburn, Maj. Gen. Gouverneur K. Warren's II Corps marched to Catlett Station along the Orange and Alexandria Railroad, then marched northward to catch up with the V Corps at Bristoe Station. Sykes became nervous, though, and left Bristoe Station before Warren fully arrived. Meanwhile, Lt. Gen. A. P. Hill's corps marched from Warrenton to Greenwich via the Warrenton Turnpike and Greenwich Road. Hill, knowing they were nearing the Army of the Potomac, pushed onward. As he approached Bristoe Station, he saw Syke's V Corps. Believing that this was the rearguard of the Army of the Potomac, the aggressive corps commander quickly ordered Maj. Gen. Henry Heth to attack. Soon, a large Federal infantry force appeared on Heth's right along the railroad. Heth had to turn to face the new threat on his flank.

As Warren and his soldiers marched north towards Bristoe Station, another large contingent of soldiers approached it from the southwest. Awaking from their bivouacs early that morning north of Warrenton along the Warrenton Turnpike, A. P. Hill and his Third Corps quickly formed in column on the road. After marching east along the Turnpike for about three miles, Hill's corps split. Receiving reports that a part of the Federal army was around Buckland, Hill dispatched his leading division under Maj. Gen. Richard Anderson towards the small village while the rest of the corps swung northeast onto Greenwich Road. When Anderson arrived near Buckland, only Federal cavalry and wagons were present. Anderson

determined there was not threat and retraced his steps and rejoined Hill.

Since there were no Federal soldiers in the immediate vicinity, Hill's wagons were ordered to park on the Warrenton Turnpike along with Brig. Gen. Alfred Scales's North Carolina brigade. Thus unimpeded by its wagon train, the march of Hill's corps quickened, increasing the chance that Hill could still intercept a part of the Army of the Potomac before it reached the fortifications at Centreville.

The first Federal soldiers Hill's troops encountered were stragglers of the Federal III Corps around the town of Greenwich. After encamping there for the night, French's soldiers followed Greenwich Road northeast, crossing Broad Run at Milford and continuing their march towards Centreville. While the majority of French's men escaped, about 150 were not so lucky and were captured by Hill.

Besides the unfortunate stragglers, Hill's soldiers also saw "guns, knapsacks, blankets, etc, strewn along the road showing that the enemy was moving in rapid retreat." Presented with this evidence of a hard-pressed foe, the Confederate pace quickened as many soldiers in the ranks thought that a repeat of the 2nd Manassas campaign was again in progress.

A few miles farther down the road, about a mile west of Bristoe Station, Hill spotted more Federal soldiers. Instead of seeing Warren's soldiers marching along the railroad, Hill instead surveyed the sprawling camp of the rearguard of the Federal V Corps under Maj. Gen. George Sykes. Sykes's men were located north of Broad Run at a small community called Milford, settled before the Civil War by New Jersey immigrants. Because of the recent prisoners, Hill thought he was looking at the rearguard of the Federal III Corps.

**After escaping converging Confederates at Auburn, Maj. Gen. Warren ordered his II Corps to halt at Cattlet's Station.** (loc)

This image from around 1912 shows Milford Mills. Sykes's V Corps was encamped around here on the early afternoon of October 14, 1863. (mm)

Maj. Gen. George Sykes commanded the V Corps. Known as "Tardy George" for often being late, he was nonetheless anxious to retreat to Centreville, abandoning the II Corps around Bristoe Station. (loc)

Earlier in the day while retreating towards Centreville, Sykes had received orders from Meade to remain at Milford until he saw the head of Warren's column, after which he could resume his retreat, though making sure to remain in supporting distance of Warren. Intently scanning the railroad for any signs of the II Corps, Sykes quickly became nervous about his position. Sending couriers to Warren asking about his progress, Sykes took time to lecture Warren about the dangers facing both corps if Warren did not arrive at Bristoe Station soon: "The longer you delay the more force they can bring against you & if Lee's army is on your left two corps are little better than one." Warren's reaction to this message is not recorded. Worried about the interval between the V and III corps, Sykes wrote Warren another dispatch: the moment he saw Warren he would continue his retreat.

While anxiously awaiting Warren, Sykes disobeyed a direct order and failed to picket the roads leading from the south and west, including the road that Hill was marching on.

A few moments after that second message was sent, one of Sykes's staff officers saw a group of mounted men along the railroad. One soldier later recalled that it made Sykes as happy as Christmas morning. Without verifying the identity of the mounted men, Sykes assumed it was the head of the II Corps and immediately ordered his corps in motion.

Though the lead elements of the II Corps were arriving, Sykes' orders required him to remain until the bulk of Warren's corpse arrived. Sykes would not be in supporting distance of Warren if trouble arose. When Warren learned that Sykes abandoned him, an officer remembered Warren exploding. "I will whip them alone, then," he vowed—adding, said the officer, "some pretty strong Saxon words."

Sykes's orders to move were just being delivered to his brigades when Hill spied them. With Federal soldiers lazily encamped along Broad Run and a large wagon train within easy striking distance, Hill decided to attack the V Corps immediately with the forces at hand: Maj. Gen. Henry Heth's division and Lt. Col. William Poague's artillery battalion. Poague's guns deployed onto the high ground south of Broad Run and artillery shells quickly rained down into the V Corps. Captain Francis Donaldson of the 118th Pennsylvania remembered the scene:

Lt. Col. William T. Poague commanded an artillery battalion in Hill's Corps. Initially positioned across from Milford Mills, Poague's artillerists would be deployed after Heth's assault. (loc)

> *Shot well directed ploughed into the crowded mass on the bluff. A stampede ensued the like I never before witnessed. So astounded were the men and so unprepared for such an attack that without waiting for orders they gathered up their traps, seized the boiling hot coffee pots, and grasping their muskets,*

On top of this hill, A. P. Hill spotted elements of Sykes's V Corps encamped by Milford. Unfortunately for Hill, the landscape also obscured the nearby railroad, which would prove disastrous for him. Today, the view is altered by a shopping center parking lot and fountain. (pg)

**Maj. Gen. Henry Heth commanded Hill's lead division. Ordered to attack nearby Federal forces, Heth quickly lost control of his command.** (loc)

*made off at a mad pace. It was a spontaneous retreat, including all branches of the service— Artillery, without attempting to reply to the enemy's fire, Cavalry, General, and Staff officers all took to their heels and beat a disgraceful retreat, crowding and pushing one another in painful disorder and eagerness to get beyond the range of the guns which plied them so unmercifully.*

With most of the Federal soldiers running from the field, Joseph K. Corson, assistant surgeon for the 6th Pennsylvania Reserves, and an unnamed assistant ran to the aid of a severely wounded soldier who had been abandoned by his comrades. Corson and his assistant survived the artillery barrage and were able to successfully evacuate the wounded man to a field station. In 1899, in recognition of this perilous act, Corson was awarded the Medal of Honor.

With Poague's guns throwing the V Corps in disorder, Hill ordered Maj. Gen. Harry Heth to deploy his division and increase the pressure on the Federals in the hopes of defeating and potentially capturing a large force of the Army of the Potomac.

Henry Heth was a relative newcomer to the Army of Northern Virginia. A native Virginian, he had served the first two years of the war in West Virginia and East Tennessee. In the spring of 1863, Heth was transferred to Lee's army and led a brigade at Chancellorsville and a division at Gettysburg. An aggressive commander, Heth had a habit of letting his command get away from him and using just a fraction of his force—a tendency he had recently demonstrated on the first day at Gettysburg. Unfortunately for the Confederate army, Heth's performance at Bristoe Station would not improve.

At the time of the Bristoe campaign, Heth led one of the strongest divisions in Lee's army. Using the Milford Road as his axis of advance, Heth deployed his division facing east towards Milford. South of the road was John R. Cooke's large North Carolina brigade, which had just recently rejoined the Army of Northern Virginia after guarding Richmond during the Gettysburg campaign. Having missed the deadly battle in Pennsylvania, Cooke's Tar Heels made up the largest brigade in Lee's army.

To the left of Cooke on the north side of the road fanned William W. Kirkland's brigade of North Carolinians. Originally commanded by J.

Johnston Pettigrew, the Tar Heels took tremendous causalities during the Gettysburg campaign, including their beloved brigade commander. While not as strong as they were in June, the return of the 44th North Carolina, which spent the summer guarding Richmond alongside Cooke's brigade, made up for many of the losses the brigade suffered.

Approximately 200 yards to the rear of Kirkland's Tar Heels was the mixed brigade of Henry Walker. By comparison to the two Tar Heel brigades, Walker's command was one of the smallest brigades in Lee's army. Made up of Alabamians, Tennesseans, and Virginians, Walker's command was created by the consolidation of the survivors of James Archer's Tennessee brigade and John Brockenbrough's Virginia brigade. While the men of Archer's brigade were seasoned veterans, Walker's Virginians had a poor reputation in the army after disappointing performances in the past. In part to have a steady hand over the brigade, Walker was promoted over Brockenbrough— leading to the latter's indigent resignation and howls of protests from the Virginians. Walker's brigade would require close supervision by their brigade and division commanders in their next battle.

Finally, held in reserve until Anderson's division

**This sketch by Alfred Waud depicts the wagon trail of the II Corps fording Kettle Run on their way to Brentsville.** (loc)

**Deploying on this ridge, Poague's Artillery Battalion quickly dominated the V Corps encamped around Milford Mills.** (pg)

appeared on the field was Joseph Davis's mixed brigade of Mississippians and North Carolinians.

Once the forward movement began, Walker's brigade had the task of extending the Confederate line by forming on the left of Kirkland's Carolinians. Unfortunately for Walker, his command was half the size of Kirkland's and had a considerable distance to travel before aligning onto Kirkland's left. Altogether, approximately 5,000 Southern infantry—which one Federal officer described as looking "gaunt and weary, and had, for the most part, a dogged air"—were in line ready to advance.

Poague's thundering shells, which sent Sykes's command scurrying northward, were the signal for Heth to begin his assault.

The artillery firing also signaled to the head of the 2nd Division of the II Corps—which was just then approaching Bristoe Station—that a sizable Confederate force was nearby. With an unknown enemy force to his left flank, division commander Brig. Gen. Alexander S. Webb ordered the 1st Minnesota, 59th New York, and 7th Michigan to the left as skirmishers to reinforce the column's flankers. Double-quicking to a slight hill a few hundred yards west of the railroad, the three regiments deployed into a loose skirmish line. The veteran Midwesterners and New Yorkers hid behind all available cover, from trees to the garbage heaps that were left behind by earlier Federal encampments. Once aligned, the skirmishers took aim at the left flank of the Confederate line and opened fire.

The target of the Federal skirmishers was Col. Edward D. Hall's 46th North Carolina, the right flank of Cooke's brigade. Surprised by Federal soldiers coming from a location initially thought clear of enemy soldiers, Hall sent word to Cooke and faced his rightmost company towards the railroad to deal with the threat. One company was no match against three Federal regiments, so Hall was forced to deploy his entire regiment towards the railroad, bending perpendicular to the main Southern line.

Hall's report of the unexpected Yankees quickly went up the chain of command. With Sykes's troops running quickly from the field, the Confederate high command altered the assault orders for Heth's division. Instead of advancing north towards Milford, Heth was to wheel his line to the east and assault the railroad with Cooke, Kirkland, and Walker.

Initially Cooke was baffled by this order to attack a completely unknown area and sent multiple couriers to Heth asking if the order was correct. Finally, one of Hill's staff officers reached the scene and demanded that the new orders were to be fulfilled at once. At the time, most Southern officers thought that the harassing Federal skirmish line was part of the same rearguard that had fled so fast from Milford. Unfortunately for Heth's soldiers, they were instead advancing towards the lead elements of the II Corps.

"By God I will carry my men in," an incredulous

**All that's left of Milford Mills in 2014. The site sits below the Chick-fil-A on Rt. 28 near Broad Run.** (pg)

Cooke exclaimed when he received orders to assault the railroad, "and when flanked I will face them about, and cut my way out."

## At Bristoe Station

While today a shopping center occupies this ridge, in 1863 it was from on top of this hill that A. P. Hill spied Federal soldiers. To your right front you will see a hill beyond the houses with a lone tree; this is where the first Federal skirmishers fired into the flank of Cooke's brigade.

The Federal V Corps was encamped north of this position at a small settlement called Milford, which was approximately located where the modern Chik-Fil-A sits along Route 28. Heth's division was initially deployed facing north, with Cooke's brigade on the right of Route 28 and Kirkland's brigade to the left, with Walker's brigade about 200 yards to his rear. Davis's brigade was held in reserve near the intersection of modern Vint Hill Road and Route 28.

Once Heth's division was in motion, Federal soldiers from the II Corps emerged to the east. While the modern housing development to the east has been raised approximately 20 feet, with the series of small ridges in between here and the railroad, it would be very difficult to make out any force marching along the railroad itself.

**Bristoe Station Battlefield Heritage Park, opened in 2007, is administered by the Prince William County Historic Preservation Division.** (cm)

In order to hasten his march, Warren ordered part of the II Corps to march in the railroad track, while the rest marched on the low hills to the east. (ro)

## ➡ To Stop 7

Exit the Bristow Center shopping center. Take a right onto Route 619 (Linton Hall Road). Drive one mile and make a right onto Iron Brigade Unit Avenue. At the traffic circle, proceed left to the Bristoe Station Battlefield Heritage Park. Once parked, walk up the paved walkway to the top of the hill.

GPS: N 38.727013, W 77.541946

# The Battle of Bristoe Station

## CHAPTER SEVEN
### Oct. 14, 1863

Writing back to his family, a Virginian "was struck with the barrenness of the country around Bristoe Station. We encountered much wire grass, broom straw, stunted pines, and other scrubby trees." Maneuvering straight through such terrain was a challenge for Heth's division, let alone pivoting 90 degrees and assaulting a different location. Having the smallest arc to travel, Cooke's brigade survived the maneuver in good order, with the left flank of the brigade guiding along the south edge of Brentsville Road.

Kirkland's brigade, having to travel a longer arc, eventually ended on the northern side of the road with the left end of the line closer to the railroad than the right. As a result of this angle, Kirkland's right-most regiment, the 44th North Carolina, soon crossed south of the road, thereby cutting off the advance of Cooke's left-most regiment, the 48th North Carolina, which took no further part in the battle.

Instead of following Kirkland's advance and extending the line to the left as ordered, Walker's brigade continued to march north towards Milford and played an insignificant part in the battle. With this being Walker's first engagement at the brigade level and the lackluster reputation of part of his brigade, it should have operated under the close eye of Heth. However there is no evidence of Heth's presence among his division after the wheeling movement, instead letting his brigade commanders act independently of one another.

With the battle being fought on the brigade level, the Tar Heels south of the road were fortunate to have John R. Cooke at the helm. Born in Missouri and raised in Virginia, Cooke was the son of Philip St. George Cooke, a

After being shot, Col. James Mallon was dragged into this creek for shelter. Unfortunately, Mallon expired within minutes. (pg)

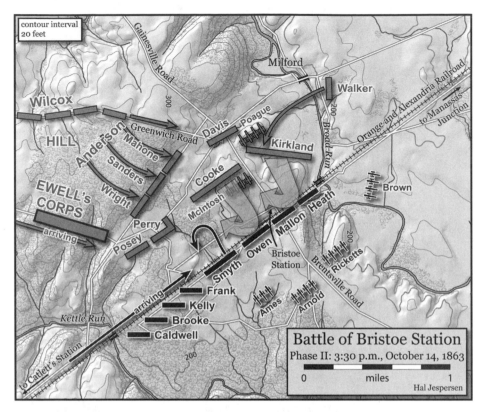

**BATTLE OF BRISTOE STATION, PHASE II**—As Maj. Gen. Henry Heth's division turned toward the railroad embankment, the Federal II Corps rushed into place. The brigades of Brig. Gen. John Cooke and Brig. Gen. William Kirkland began to advance against the Federals, but took heavy casualties. Soon a Confederate artillery battery under Maj. David McIntosh arrived, personally positioned by Lt. Gen. A. P. Hill. As the brigades of Cooke and Kirkland stalled in their attack, they were forced from the field, thus leaving McIntosh's artillery unprotected. Adventurous Federals advanced and captured five Confederate artillery pieces. Although the initial attack was a disaster, the rest of Hill's corps soon arrived and began to deploy.

U.S. Army officer who remained loyal to the Union during the Civil War, and brother-in-law to J. E. B. Stuart. A Harvard graduate, Cooke entered the U.S. Army prior the war but resigned his commission when Virginia seceded. Performing admirably during the first half of the war, Cooke was rewarded with the promotion to Brig. general nearly a year before Bristoe Station. Wounded while fighting at Marye's Heights during the battle of Fredericksburg, Cooke quickly recovered and, by October 1863, had transformed his four regiments from the Old North State into a solid brigade.

North of the road, commanding the Carolinians of the old Pettigrew Brigade was Brig. Gen. William W. Kirkland. A North Carolinian by birth, Kirkland attended West Point but failed to graduate, and instead became an officer in the United States Marine Corps. Resigning from the Marines prior to the secession crisis, Kirkland began the war commanding the 21st North Carolina. While recuperating from a wound he suffered at the first battle of Winchester, Kirkland served in Tennessee as chief of staff to Maj. Gen. Patrick Cleburne during the battle of Murfreesboro. Rejoining his regiment in the spring of 1863, Kirkland fought at Gettysburg. During the reorganization of Lee's army in the late summer of 1863, Kirkland was promoted to brigade command and replaced the popular Pettigrew. For the most part, Cooke's and Kirkland's regiments were commanded by seasoned, veteran officers.

One of the popular misconceptions about the battle of Bristoe Station is that Hill's Confederates attacked the entire Federal II Corps posted safely behind the railroad embankment. While all of the II Corps were on the field by the end of the battle, when Heth's Tar Heels initially charged towards the railroad, they actually outnumbered their Federal counterparts. Warren had halted his soldiers at Catlett Station to consolidate his troops on the march towards Centreville, but the rapid gait on top of railroad ties had again stretched his corps. Attempts to divert

**Because the right of the Federal line did not rest on Broad Run, the 11th North Carolina was able to temporarily break through the railroad here. Intense artillery and rifle fire drove them back.** (pg)

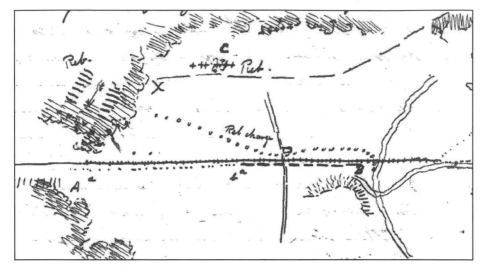

**Brig. Gen. Alexander Webb commanded the Second Division of the II Corps during the Bristoe campaign. In a letter, he drew this map of the Bristoe Station battlefield.** (yl)

**During the height of the battle, Col. Mallon was mortally wounded while on his way to check on his close friend, Henry Abbott.** (loc)

some columns along the many farm lanes running perpendicular to the railroad alleviated congestion of the main route, but the II Corps's three divisions was still badly separated from one another as they arrived on the field.

Two brigades, Col. Francis E. Heath's and Col. James E. Mallon's from Alexander Webb's division, were at the head of the column and were marching on the railroad bed itself. They could easily fight within the protection of its embankments and cuts within moments. A few hundred yards to their rear and marching on a farm road a little east of the railroad were the brigades of Brig. Gen. Joshua T. Owen and Col. Thomas A. Smyth of Brig. Gen. Alexander Hays's division, which had to cover approximately 300 yards of open ground before reaching the protection of the main line.

Altogether, the four brigades of blue-coated soldiers numbered approximately 4,300 men. While outnumbered by the rebels by about 800 men, the strong position in the railroad would more than make up for the numerical disparity, provided that all four brigades reached the position before the Tar Heels did.

The key for victory at Bristoe Station was possession of the railroad. Every second the Southerners were delayed in their assault, more and more Federal soldiers reinforced the main line.

The first Federals that Confederates encountered were the skirmishers that had forced the Confederate wheel. To the men from Minnesota, Michigan, and New York, the advancing Confederate line looked like "a million of them." Veterans of some of the bloodiest fighting of the war, the soldiers on the Federal skirmish line understood it was suicidal to try and resist the assault on their own and quickly began running back to the protection of the railroad, stopping briefly to fire their rifles at the rebels before continuing their retreat. James Wright of the 1st Minnesota remembered that

> The bullets fairly sizzled as they passed over us, and some of them struck the ground beside us, making the dirt fly and glancing away with a peculiar whining sound I never heard on any other occasion. As we were going down the hill, a large proportion of their bullets passed over us, as was evident from the little puffs of dust rising in front of us.

By the time the Federal skirmish line was falling back, Warren was taking control of the field. Heath's and Mallon's brigades were already in position in the railroad. Heath's line did not extend to Broad Run, creating a dangerous gap in the Federal line, and Mallon's brigade was outflanked to their left by the oncoming Carolinians. To extend the Federal line south of Mallon, Warren ordered Hays's brigades into line as fast as possible, throwing each regiment into the line as quickly as they entered the field.

In addition to the infantrymen quickly extending the line, Warren had three veteran artillery batteries soon in position. On a slight hill north of Broad Run in perfect position to enfilade the approaching Rebel line were four 12-pound Napoleons commanded by Lt. T. Frederick Brown. Immediately south of Broad Run from Brown, Capt. R. Bruce Ricketts's 3-inch rifles deployed on a slight ridge. Still farther south, Capt. William Arnold's Battery unlimbered their 3-inch rifles. Altogether, 14 Federal cannon awaited the charging Southerners.

The fire from the four batteries, along with the musketry from the retreating skirmish line, produced the first Confederate casualties of the battle. Unfortunately for the Rebels, one of the first men struck was Brig. General Cooke. A small piece of Northern lead hit Cooke's shinbone, shattering the bone. With the experienced Cooke out of the fight, command of the brigade fell upon Colonel Hall of the 46th North Carolina, which one Tar Heel felt was "quite a fall to come down from General C to such a man as Col Hall."

Around the same time that Cooke was hit, north

**Men of Owen's Brigade were positioned behind the railroad embankment here, with supporting artillery under Arnold on the heights in the distance.** (pg)

of the road Brig. General Kirkland also went down with a serious wound. Command of the brigade passed to Col. Thomas Singletary of the 44th North Carolina. The presence of both commanders would be sorely missed.

With both brigade commanders down, command and control over the Carolinians ceased to exist. Since Webb's two brigades were hidden in the railroad and Hays's brigades had yet to come up, the only Federals visible to the Rebels were the skirmishers retreating before them and the artillery batteries on the other side of the railroad. The thought of capturing what appeared to be unsupported cannon was too much to pass up, so Cooke's and Kirkland's men began a steady fire while they continued to advance. A soldier in the 44th North Carolina remembered his comrades yelling out "Kill the horses! Damn you shoot! Give them hell! Kill the gunners! Kill! Kill!" as they fired towards the Federal artillery. While a few rebel musket balls found their mark against the artillerists and their horses, the main result of this fire was to slow down the Carolinians' attack.

After a few rounds were fired at the Federal artillery, Hays's two brigades emerged into view as they ran to the protection of the main Federal line. Seeing hundreds of Federal infantrymen appear out of nowhere, the Tar Heels shifted their fire to this unexpected target. It was during this race to the railroad that most of the Federal killed and wounded occurred. Of the approximate 300 Federal casualties sustained at Bristoe Station, nearly half belonged to Brig. General Owen's four New York regiments as they ran towards the railroad. In the space of about five minutes—the time it took to reach the railroad—Owen's brigade saw about 80 men go down. Once in the protection of the railroad, only a few more soldiers would be unfortunate enough to be shot.

Hays's brigades, once they got into position, extended the Federal line south. Then the entire Federal line "sent into the forces of the advancing, yelling Rebels a perfect hurricane of shot." Heth's brigades were about 200 yards from the Federals when they were slammed with this fire, momentarily halting their advance on the slight hill that led to the railroad.

Realizing that to stay in their current position meant annihilation, and with no orders on what to do, Col. George Whitfield of the 27th North Carolina found his acting brigade commander and suggested

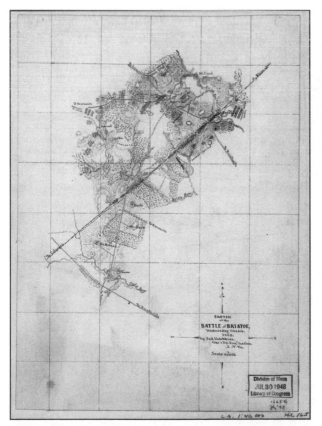

Completed after the campaign, this map by Jedidiah Hotchkiss shows the positions of both armies at Bristoe Station near the end of the fighting. Hotchkiss was not present at the battle and made the map based off of first-hand accounts. (loc)

that they either retreat or continue to advance. Hall replied that "we would have to charge them."

After the battle, Hall would argue that he intended for the entire brigade to advance together. However, due to the din and confusion of battle, Colonel Whitfield thought that he was to advance his regiment immediately without waiting for the other regiments. To make matters worse, when the individual companies of the 27th North Carolina received the order to charge, they executed it piecemeal. "In a moment," remembered John Sloan after relaying the order to charge, "we were double-quicking down the hill, our men falling at every step."

The roar of cannon and the rattle of musketry tore holes in the entire Southern line, but the 27th North Carolina, charging alone, took the majority of fire. About 70 yards away from the Unionists stood the remains of the farm of Thomas Davis. Running to the protection of a few outbuildings, once the Tar Heels reached the Davis farm they could go no farther.

Dozens of Confederates went down as the Federal line erupted in an even heavier fire. The fire was so severe that it stopped the other regiments of Cooke's brigade in a ditch about 40 yards away from the Davis farm. The Confederate

**Marching near a ridge east of the railroad, Owen's brigade of New Yorkers had to advance over open ground to reach the protection of the cut. They suffered the majority of their casualties during this charge.** (es)

assault south of Brentsville road had reached its high water mark.

North of the road, the Confederate assault was having better luck. Instead of one slight hill such as the one that Cooke's men maneuvered over, the land Kirkland's soldiers charged over was a series of small ridges and valleys. While the terrain slowed the progress of the assault, it gave the Confederates some cover. Like Cooke's brigade, Kirkland's regiments fought independently of another. The 44th North Carolina stopped their advance about 70 yards from the railroad, while the 47th North Carolina stopped once they reached a series of old camp huts built by Federal soldiers earlier in the war. The left-most regiments—the 11th and 52nd North Carolina—exploited the gap in the Federal line and actually reached the railroad, between Broad Run and Heath's brigade.

Seeing gray soldiers in the railroad, Brown had his guns wheeled towards the railroad and soon his battery shot canister into the Tar Heels left and rear. With fire soon coming from their right from the 19th Maine, the Carolinians were being shot from all sides and quickly fell back to the relative protection of the abandoned huts they had passed earlier.

A little farther to the south, the 26th North Carolina was also able to breach the Federal line. The Carolinians hit the line manned by the 42nd New York, posted along the flat ground where the railroad and Brentsville road intersected. In addition to having very little protection, the 42nd New York had received a large amount of recruits and draftees in the weeks leading up to Bristoe Station. The charge of the veteran Tar Heels was too much, and the New Yorkers quickly broke to the rear, allowing the Southerners a small toehold onto the line.

With the collapse of the New Yorkers, Col. James Mallon, acting brigade commander, jumped into action. Born to Irish parents in Brooklyn,

This sketch by Alfred Waud shows Federal artillery in action at Bristoe. This view is from the modern day VRE parking lot towards the battlefield park. (loc)

**While the majority of Warren's command was engaged in the railroad, the tiny 10th New York infantry was positioned near these ridges in support of the two batteries.** (pg)

Mallon worked in various New York City wholesale commission businesses before creating his own. A prewar member of the elite 7th New York National Guard, when hostilities broke out Mallon joined the 42nd New York, rising from the rank of lieutenant to colonel. Assigned to New York after Gettysburg to obtain recruits and conscripts for his regiment, Mallon had been anxious to return to the army so as to be with his men in the next fight.

Mallon was able to get his soldiers in order, and soon such a heavy fire was directed towards the 26th North Carolina that the Tar Heels were forced to fall back, leaving the intersection to the Yankees.

With Confederates in his front retreating, Mallon soon became worried about the welfare of his good friend, Maj. Henry Abbott of the 20th Massachusetts, who was a little further up the line. Ignoring the protests of several of his staff officers, Mallon started walking up the line, exposing himself to enemy fire. Soon a rebel Minnie ball slammed into Mallon's stomach, mortally wounding the New Yorker. "It was terrible blow," Abbott later said of his friend's death, "but it seems almost as if one were destined to be calloused by these repeated losses of the best and noblest." Mallon was the highest-ranking Federal causality at Bristoe Station.

With the two breaches sealed, the fire from the Federal line intensified along Heth's front. Fighting for their lives, a Carolinian remembered "nearly every man of strong voice was bawling out something of which I could distinguish the following: 'Cease Fire,' 'Lie down,' 'Don't shoot, you are shooting our own men,' 'Charge!' 'Fall Back!' and the like, so that it was impossible to recognize the voice of our commander unless very near him."

Soon small bands of Confederate soldiers were retreating. Realizing that to stay in their position meant destruction, staff officers ran to the various regiments to order the retreat. One Tar Heel saw a comrade get hit by a Minnie ball in the stomach, which to him sounded like "the striking of swift baseball on a catcher's glove." Soon a team of stretcher bearers arrived and were evacuating him to the rear towards a field hospital, when a musket ball hit one of the bearers, killing him instantly and throwing the wounded man on the ground. With the fire too intense to retrieve him, the surviving stretcher bearers continued their way to the rear.

South of Brentsville Road, the advanced position of the 27th North Carolina made any retreat from the Davis farm a very dangerous gambit. Fortunately their comrades in the 15th North Carolina were able to provide enough covering fire that the soldiers around the Davis buildings had a slightly better chance of safety during their retreat. Like Kirkland's brigade, once Cooke's regiments began to retreat, almost all unit cohesion was lost, save for the 15th North Carolina, which stayed relatively intact in their withdrawal.

From the wheeling movement to the assault and, finally, to the retreat from the railroad, the Confederate attack took at most 45 minutes. Looking over the ground where the Carolinians had fought, one Federal officer remembered, "The slope of the plain over which the enemy charged was covered with killed and wounded, and the cries and groans of the latter were distressing."

Even though the Tar Heel assault was finished, the sun had not set, and more fighting was in store in the fields around Bristoe Station.

*At Bristoe Station Battlefield Heritage Park*

From atop this hill you can see the gentle slope down towards the railroad that Cooke's North Carolinians advanced over in 1863. Once Cooke's men had charged, A. P. Hill ordered David McIntosh's artillery battalion to deploy on this hill to provide support for the infantry. Unfortunately for McIntosh, his support was supposed to be Cooke's regiments, though no one ever relayed that information to the Tar Heels. When the infantrymen retreated, they continued past this hill, sweeping some of the artillerists with them. Federal skirmishers quickly took advantage of the situation and captured five cannons that were left here.

If you walk down the trail towards the railroad, you will come to the Robinson Family cemetery. In 1863, this was the location of the Davis farm. Thomas Davis was the sheriff for Prince William County prior to the war and an ardent Unionist. During the battle of Kettle Run in August 1862, Davis evacuated his family to Brentsville four miles away. When he returned, he found that his house had been converted into a Federal field hospital. Davis remained in Prince William County until September 1863 when he received word that some of his Confederate neighbors were planning on arresting him and sending him to Richmond. Fleeing with his family to Washington, D.C., Davis did not return to his farm until after the war. When he returned, he discovered that all his buildings were completely demolished. Because of the hard soil in Prince William County and with a large open space in the middle of a field after the war, this is probably one of the reasons that the Robinson family cemetery is located here.

## ➡️ To Stop 8

*Continue walking the "Bristoe 1863" Trail throughout the park. If you have time and are interested, walk the trail covering the winter encampment of "Camp Jones" and the August 27, 1862, battle of Kettle Run. This trail leaves from the parking lot.*

*Only 25 percent of the battlefield is currently preserved in the park. To visit some of the battlefield locations outside the park, follow the instructions below.*

Today the Robertson Cemetery, established in the 1880s, sits near the same location of the T.K. Davis home site during the battle. (pg)

Exit the Park and turn right onto Bristow Road (Rt. 619) You are driving in the direction of the Confederate attack, with Cooke's brigade on your right and Kirkland's brigade on your left. As you cross the railroad, you are in the approximate area where the 26th North Carolina was able to temporarily breach the line. Turn right onto Valley View Road and pull into the United States Post Office on your left. Looking to the west towards the park, you will notice a ridge on the other side of the road where Arnold's six Napoleons were deployed during the battle.

Retrace your route by taking a right onto Valley View Road and take a left onto Bristow Road. On your right is the ridge where Rickett's six guns were positioned on the afternoon of October 14.

After you have passed the park, take a right onto Chapel Springs Road. At the stop sign, turn right onto Nokesville Road (Route 28). You are now heading in the direction Walker's wayward brigade went.

At the first traffic light, turn right onto Piper Lane. You will now be paralleling Broad Run. After you pass under the railroad, turn left and drive to the VRE station lot. Facing the VRE lot is where the windmill in the Alfred Waud drawing was located. To your rear, Brown's Rhode Island battery was positioned. Later that night, elements of the returned V Corps would be positioned in front of you behind the railroad.

Proceed back to Piper Lane. Take a right onto Piper Lane and travel back to the intersection of Piper Land and Nokesville Road. At the traffic light, continue straight. Take a left towards Chick-Fil-A. You are now in the location of the small village of Milford. The sloping hill to the north of you would have been crowded with soldiers from the V Corps in 1863. However, a few Confederate artillery shells were able to drive them northward. Return to the Bristoe Station Battlefield Heritage Park parking lot to continue.

# The Battle of Bristoe Station Part II: "Bury These Poor Men"

## CHAPTER EIGHT
### OCTOBER 14, 1863

In the midst of Kirkland and Cooke's attack against the railroad, Hill hurriedly sent for even more soldiers to throw into the fight. Poague's artillery battalion was shifted from the ridge overlooking Milford to a small hill near the Gaines family cemetery behind Kirkland's brigade. Also, Walker's wandering soldiers were finally recalled after crossing north of Broad Run. Fording Broad Run yet again, Walker's men lay down behind the cannon as support.

South of the road, Hill ordered Maj. David McIntosh's artillery battalion to a ridge about 600 yards away from the railroad. McIntosh vehemently protested the order, believing his guns would be positioned too close to the enemy without adequate support. Like Cooke's earlier reservations about an order, McIntosh's objections were ignored, and he was directed to fulfill the order. Hill hoped that McIntosh's seven guns, firing over the heads of Cooke's advancing men, could literally blow a hole in the Federal line.

McIntosh's guns were still in the process of unlimbering when shells from the three Northern batteries started to fall in their midst. McIntosh quickly became the primary target of the Yankee artillerists, and an intense converging fire turned his position into a living hell. With men, horses, and even the cannons themselves being hit by Federal shells, McIntosh's gunners tried to respond to this tempest of lead and iron, but were overmatched from the beginning. When Cooke's retreating Carolinians reached the guns, the gunners were swept up in the retreat, and seven abandoned guns beckoned the Yankee soldiers.

One of the controversies that arose from the battle

McIntosh lost five cannon at Bristoe, prompting one Richmond newspaper editor to acidly describe it as "the first time in history that a retreating army captured cannon from an attacking army." (pg)

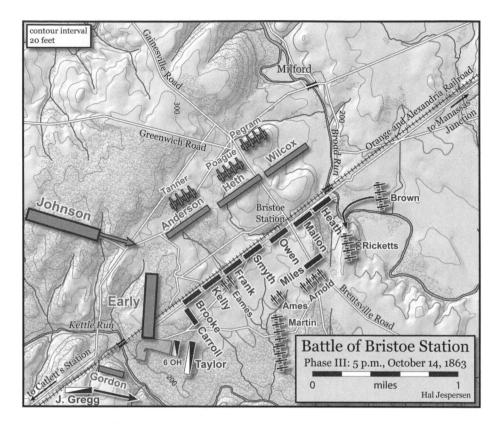

**BATTLE OF BRISTOE STATION, PHASE III**—By 4 p.m., all of Hill's corps was on the field, but he made no attempts to renew the attack. An artillery duel took place that mortally wounded Brig. Gen. Carnot Posey. By 5 p.m., Lt. Gen. Richard Ewell's men arrived with Gen. Robert E. Lee. Hill pointed out to Ewell the opportunity to crush a Federal corps, and Ewell ordered his men into place. Maj. Gen. Jubal Early was ordered to straddle the railroad and flank the Federals, but Early would not attack unless he had his whole division. Brigadier General John Gordon's brigade was missing, chasing the Federal supply train and Federal cavalry. Soon, sunset ended any chance of a Confederate attack, and the Federal II Corps marched away to Centreville under the cover of darkness.

was who was at fault for the loss of McIntosh's guns. The guns had been assigned to Maj. General Anderson's division, so ideally, any infantry support for the Alabamian's guns would come from one of Anderson's brigades. So urgent was the need for artillery support, though, that Hill had forwarded McIntosh into position while the rest of Anderson's soldiers were still marching to the battlefield. However, Davis's brigade of Mississippians and North Carolinians were still in reserve about 300 yards in rear of the artillerists. It is still unclear why, but evidence suggests that Hill considered Cooke's four regiments battling for their lives near the railroad track adequate support for McIntosh. Added to

this blunder, it seems that no staff officers ventured to Cooke's brigade to tell them of the guns to their rear. When McIntosh's guns opened fire, it appears that their sound mixed together with the roar of the Federal guns and musketry. Thus, the first time that many of Cooke's men knew of McIntosh's presence was when they ran between the guns. Regardless of fault, after Cooke's men had withdrawn from the field, seven abandoned pieces of artillery stood within sight of hundreds of Federal soldiers.

The trophies proved too tempting, and soon small squads of Federal soldiers were cautiously advancing towards the guns on their own initiative. Some slight controversy arose later on concerning which particular regiment should be given the honor of capturing the guns. In truth, every regiment then deployed in the railroad had at least a few soldiers advancing up towards the Confederate guns.

A few yards from the main line, these soldiers quickly encountered scores of Carolinians who had decided against trying their luck in retreating, hunkered down instead in whatever protection they could find. Soon, hundreds of captured Confederates were escorted back to the railroad.

Finally reaching the location of the batteries, a Federal officer remembered seeing "within the space of an acre lie twenty-one dead animals." With so many of the artillery horses killed, the Federal soldiers slowly started manhandling the cannon back down towards the railroad. Although seven guns were on the hill, two were too badly damaged to move. As a Richmond newspaper editor later quipped, it was the

**Federal counterbattery fire was so intense that McIntosh's Battery lost the majority of their horses killed or wounded. Without horses, the guns were immobile.** (loc)

**On the evening of October 14th, the entire II Corps quietly crossed Broad Run here and headed to Centreville.** (pg)

first time in recorded military history that a retreating army captured artillery from an attacking force.

At the same time that these small squads of Federals were cautiously advancing towards the guns, Col. Thomas Smyth's entire brigade advanced towards the retreating Confederates. The reason for this lone foray is unclear, though there is some evidence that Hays told his Brig.s to counterattack any Confederate assault immediately. Pushing into a dense pine thicket, Smyth's men continued to advance until they saw Confederate soldiers headed straight at them.

The Rebels that Smyth's men saw were the fresh brigades of Brig. Gen. Carnot Posey's Mississippians and Brig. Gen. Edward Perry's Floridians, who had all just recently arrived onto the field. Too late to join the assault on the railroad, Perry's and Posey's brigades delivered some long-range fire towards Smyth's men, which was enough resistance to send the Yankees back to the protection of the embankment.

With the Federals no longer an immediate threat, the Floridians and Mississippians laid down to shield themselves from the occasional artillery shell sent their way. After a few moments, one shell exploded by Posey, shrapnel tearing into his left thigh. Posey was soon evacuated to Charlottesville, where he had attended law school in his youth. Initially thought to be a minor though painful

After Perry's and Posey's slight brush with the Federals, both sides were content to wait for the rest of their commands to come up before renewing the fight. Soon, Brig. Gen. John Caldwell's division arrived on the field, bringing the II Corps to full strength. A few moments later, the rest of Hill's corps also deployed on the battlefield. Some slight skirmishing occurred between the two lines but soon a lull came over the field.

In 1863, when Smyth's brigade engaged in a counterattack on Hill's retreating troops, this field was covered in thick scrub brush. (ro)

wound, it soon became infected. Posey eventually succumbed to the injury almost a month after the battle, becoming the highest-ranking Confederate casualty of Bristoe Station.

*    *    *

Around 6:00 p.m., Ewell's corps started streaming into position, thus uniting the entire Army of Northern Virginia—approximately 40,000 men. Vastly outnumbering the 11,000 Federals behind the railroad, Lee's army only had a few more moments of sunlight before the sun set and the fighting would be over. Johnson's division extended Hill's line to the south, while Early's division swung into position to try and outflank the II Corps from the railroad.

The first of Early's brigades to reach the field, Brig. General Gordon's Georgia brigade, started to skirmish with the Federals after seeing a few Federal wagons in the distance. Moving forward alone,

Here in what today is a modern housing development, Brig. Gen. Carnot Posey was deploying his brigade of Mississippians when a stray Federal artillery shell exploded, mortally wounding him. (pg)

Gordon realized that he was facing a larger force than he expected and was content to skirmish until the rest of Early's division was in position.

Unfortunately, Early had earlier ordered Gordon to stay in place while he went back to retrieve his other two brigades. Arriving on the field with the balance of his division, Early searched in vain for Gordon. With the elusive Georgian nowhere to be seen, Early hesitated to deploy all his men in a position that could have rolled up the entire Federal position.

During this same time, Confederates were picking up many Federal stragglers along the railroad. A brave charge by the 6th Ohio cavalry freed many of these men. The Ohioans were part of Taylor's cavalry brigade and served as the far left of Warren's line. This short but bold attack also delayed Early's ability to put his men in position. By the time Early was set to attack the refused right flank of the II Corps, twilight quickly brought an end to the fighting.

While a division of the V Corps returned to link up with Warren during the early evening, the II Corps commander knew that we has now facing the entire Rebel army, and to stay until morning risked the destruction of his entire command. Gathering up his wounded, Warren first sent those men along the railroad towards Centreville. At midnight, orders were delivered that set the rest of the Federal soldiers in motion. Clutching accoutrements to silence their withdrawal, by dawn the rear elements of the II Corps were finally filing into the fortifications at Centreville.

The last chance to defeat Meade's army had slipped away.

Altogether the fighting at Bristoe Station was small compared to other Civil War battles. For the regiments that saw combat, particularly Cooke's and Kirkland's brigades, Bristoe Station was as horrendous as any fighting they had experienced during the war.

After taking a severe pounding at Gettysburg, Kirkland's brigade lost nearly 600 more irreplaceable men. Some units were almost annihilated. Company F of the 26th North Carolina went into the fight at Bristoe Station with 34 men and lost 32.

South of the road, Cooke's brigade took equally heavy casualties. Seven hundred Tar Heels in Cooke's regiments were killed, wounded, or captured. The hardest hit was the 27th North Carolina, which went into the battle with 475 officers and men lost 30 men killed and 174 wounded. Company B, the Guilford Grays, went into the fight with 63 men and lost 43.

During the fight at Bristoe, Warren continuously rode his line. This Alfred Waud sketch shows Warren observing Brown's artillery battery. (loc)

**Brentsville was the county seat of Prince William County during the 19th century. Here Brig. Gen. John Buford's cavalry protected the Army of the Potomac wagon train. He nervously awaited orders to move north on the evening of the 14th, fearing a Confederate cavalry attack. Today the village is a county-owned historic site. (pg)**

The next morning, while riding over the field, Lee told Hill, "Well, well, general, bury these poor men and let us say no more about it." That's the commonly told story, anyway. But a Confederate officer remembered another exchange between Lee and Hill on the 15th—one that is probably closer to the truth.

Riding up to Lee, Hill started to apologize for the previous day, saying it was his fault. "Yes, it is your fault," Lee snapped in reply. "You committed a great blunder yesterday. Your battle line was too short, too thin and your reserves were too far behind." Then he galloped away from a crestfallen Hill.

Hill's humiliation didn't end there. A few weeks later, Warren sent a personal note to the Confederate

**"I placed my battery in position . . . on a hill near the railroad bridge crossing Broad Run," wrote R. Bruce Ricketts, "and opened on a column of infantry near the railroad with canister and shrapnel until they broke." (ro)**

general. Before the war, Hill had courted a woman named Emily Chase, whom Warren had recently married. Warren took the fight at Bristoe as an excuse to crow: "I have not only whipped you but married your old sweetheart."

With his victory at Bristoe now added to his heroics at Gettysburg, it seemed Warren's star continued to shine. Not only did he extricate his command from a very dangerous position, he captured nearly 500 prisoners, five cannon, and three battle flags while losing 380 men at both Auburn and Bristoe Station.

The fighting at Bristoe Station was the culmination of the campaign, but it did not mark the end of the maneuvering and fighting, more of which was in store for both armies in the coming weeks.

 ## To Stop 9

*From the park's parking lot, take a right onto Iron Brigade Unit Avenue. Then take a left onto Bristow Road (Rt. 619). Stay straight onto Linton Hall Road for approximately six miles. Take Lee Highway (Rt. 29) west towards Warrenton. Drive approximately three and a half miles and turn right onto Buckland Mill Road. The Buckland Post Office is the second building on your right.*

GPS: N 38.781215, W 77.673801

**After Kirkland's Brigade was repulsed, Poague's artillery and Walker's wayward brigade redeployed on the ridge overlooking the Gaines Family cemetery.** (pg)

# The Battle of Buckland Mills

## CHAPTER NINE
### October 15-19, 1863

The morning of October 15, 1863, revealed the entire Army of the Potomac safely entrenched in the fortifications around the heights at Centreville. While the battle at Bristoe Station had created a scare within the high command, with the entire army now concentrated and positioned in such a strong location, Major General Meade was content to await the Army of Northern Virginia's next move.

Maj. General Jeb Stuart's cavalry probed along Bull Run to find a weakness. With some minor skirmishing, Stuart attempted to turn the Federal western flank. Meade was prepared for such an attempt, though, and Stuart returned to the Bristoe area.

After riding over the battlefield at Bristoe Station, Lee considered his options. The fighting on October 14 was Lee's last opportunity to engage the enemy in a position that was favorable to the Confederacy. Now with Meade at Centreville, Lee's options were limited.

First he could try and assault the earthworks and drive Meade into Washington. However, the combat at Bristoe Station showed that fighting just a portion of the Federal army behind temporary entrenchments was costly. Not only was Meade's line at Centreville stronger than Warren's ad hoc position, but if Lee was successful in driving Meade east, it would be only into the even more formidable fortifications surrounding Washington.

Another option for Lee was to continue to drive northward, as he had done before. However since Meade was so close to Lee's existing supply line, the Orange & Alexandria Railroad, any northern movement necessitated Lee changing

Although generally forgotten, the battle of Buckland Mills is commemorated by a state historical marker. (pg)

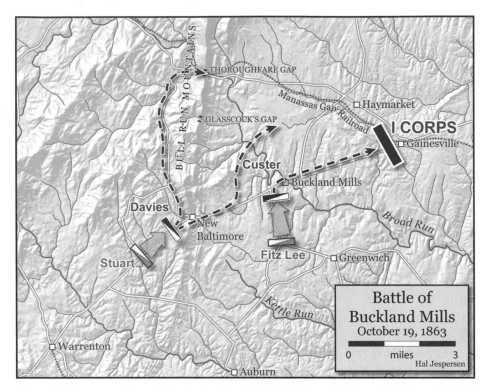

**BATTLE OF BUCKLAND MILLS**—After the battle of Bristoe Station, the Army of Northern Virginia remained in Prince William County for two days before deciding to return to Culpeper. Meade slowly pursued and sent his cavalry to find them. Near Gainesville, Brig. Gen. Judson Kilpatrick's Federal cavalry division ran into Confederate cavalry under Maj. Gen. Jeb Stuart at Buckland Mills. Forced under pressure to pull back, Stuart concocted a plan to withdraw to New Baltimore, luring Kilpatrick southward along the Warrenton Turnpike—allowing Maj. Gen. Fitzhugh Lee to attack Kilpatrick from the rear and cut off his retreat across Broad Run at Buckland Mills. Although the plan works, Brig. Gen. George Custer's brigade remained at Buckland and was able to fight off Lee briefly, giving some reprieve to the retreating Federal cavalry. Kilpatrick's cavalry scattered in the face of Stuart's cavalry and rendezvoused in Haymarket.

his logistical network to the Shenandoah Valley, a time-consuming process.

Alternatively, Lee could remain in Northern Virginia, alleviating the farms around the Rappahannock and Rapidan rivers from the presence of two armies. Unfortunately for the Confederates, three years of war had devastated the farms in Northern Virginia to the point that, to supply his army, Lee was solely reliant on the single-track O & A. During their retreat the Federals had damaged key bridges along the railroad, such as the bridge over the Rappahannock River. These bridge repairs required time to complete, further decreasing the amount of supplies reaching Lee's army.

Faced with these unsavory options, Lee ultimately decided to retreat south, destroying as much of the railroad as possible in the hopes of delaying any Federal pursuit.

In order to trick the Federals into believing that the Confederate army still lurked in force around Centreville, Lee ordered Jeb Stuart to make a "bold demonstration" with his cavalry. Harassing Meade's army at several points, Stuart successfully accomplished his mission, keeping the Federals in their entrenchments while Lee's infantrymen tore up the tracks from Manassas to the Rappahannock River. With the Rebel army slowly making its way southward, by October 18 Stuart learned that he was to follow the main army and serve as its rearguard.

*   *   *

While disaster had not befallen the Federal army thus far during the Bristoe Station maneuvers, there had been enough close calls to make Meade's pursuit of Lee a cautious one. In a dispatch to Washington on October 15, Meade estimated that Lee's force numbered about 80,000 men, nearly double the actual Confederates strength. A reply from Lincoln chastised Meade, saying "reports from Richmond make Lee's present force only 55,000." After Meade's deliberate pursuit of Lee after Gettysburg, there was fear in the Lincoln administration that Meade would again underperform. Realizing that his tenure as commander of the Army of the Potomac potentially hung on this performance, on October 18 Meade ordered his army in pursuit.

The town of Buckland in 2014. Sitting on the Prince William/Fauquier County line, Buckland was an important stop on the Warrenton Turnpike. (bps)

Leading the Federal pursuit were the horsemen of the army's Cavalry Corps, with Brig. General Kilpatrick's division riding southwest along the Warrenton Turnpike. While holding a brigade in reserve, Kilpatrick ordered his two remaining brigades to clear the Warrenton Turnpike from Centreville to Warrenton.

Brushing aside small squads of Confederate cavalrymen, on October 19 Kilpatrick cleared the Turnpike all the way to the small town of Buckland, which straddled the Prince William/Fauquier county line. The night before, Stuart had crossed his division to the south of the rain-swollen Broad Run. Posting sharpshooters in the town buildings south of the stream, the Federals had to negotiate this natural barrier under fire if they were to drive the Confederates away.

The men tasked with driving Stuart out of Buckland were Brig. Gen. George Custer and his Michigan Brigade. At the beginning of the battle, Custer and his staff rode to the stone bridge over Broad Run, close to the Confederate line. Spotting a tempting target of officers, Southern artillery posted on the heights behind the village soon started to shell the crowd of horsemen. Soon, one Confederate shell landed in the midst of the group but failed to explode. After such a close call, Custer and his staff officers rode to the safety of the rear to finish their troop deployment.

Custer ultimately decided to try and pin the Confederates in place while he outflanked their position. He positioned the 6th Michigan Cavalry astride the road with the 5th Michigan Cavalry to their right and 7th Michigan Cavalry to their left. Using the superior firepower of their Spencer carbines to hold the Confederates in their position, Custer extended his line and soon had his Wolverines on both Confederate flanks. With Wolverines splashing down into Broad Run and running up the other bank, Stuart ordered his cavalrymen to remount and ride south to Warrenton.

The sight of Stuart retreating sent a shock of elation through Kilpatrick's staff. In order to continue the momentum gained at Buckland, Kilpatrick quickly ordered his two brigades into pursuit. Brig. General Henry Davies's mixed brigade of New York, Pennsylvania, and West Virginia cavalrymen were ordered to the front, followed by Custer's Wolverines. Custer, however, refused to his move his brigade out of Buckland until his men had time to eat the breakfast delayed by the fighting. Until Custer's men and horses had had their food, Kilpatrick would pursue an entire Confederate division with just one brigade.

Unbeknownst to any of the Federals, instead of chasing Stuart to Warrenton they were trotting into a trap. While Stuart's division was retreating along the Warrenton Turnpike, Maj. Gen. Fitzhugh Lee's division was encamped to the south near Auburn. Hearing of the Confederate retreat from Buckland, Fitz Lee sensed an opportunity to destroy the Yankee division.

While Stuart lured Kilpatrick closer to Warrenton, Fitz Lee was to march his men cross country behind the Federals, retake the town of Buckland, and cut the Federal cavalrymen off from retreat. Meanwhile Stuart was to reorganize his men and lead a counterattack. If all went according to plan, Stuart would be the hammer driving Kilpatrick's men into Fitz Lee's anvil.

Riding cross country to Buckland, Fitz Lee's men encountered not the abandoned town of Buckland, but Custer's entire brigade, which was finally beginning to move out in support of Davies. Fitz Lee's lead brigade of Virginians, under Col. Thomas Owen, were surprised at the sight.

The 6th Michigan Cavalry had marched only about 300 yards when they, in turn, noticed the unknown riders in the distance. At first some soldiers thought the cavalrymen were members of the 7th Michigan Cavalry that Custer had sent to the Federal left, although some suspicious Wolverines thought that the figures were Confederates. The argument about the identity of the men continued until a puff of smoke was seen from the distant riders. Soon a bullet lodged itself in the breast of one of the lead Michigan horses, thus settling the identity of the men. With unexpected Confederate soldiers coming out of the woods to the south, Custer immediately halted his brigade and prepared to hold the Buckland bridge, Kilpatrick's sole escape route, as long as possible.

The firing to their rear came as a rude surprise

**This wartime sketch depicts Union infantrymen fording Broad Run at Buckland during the Bristoe campaign. (loc)**

This sketch by Alfred Waud depicts Union artillery deployed on the ridge north of Buckland. The town can be seen in the distance. (loc)

Brig. Gen. Henry Davies, Jr., commanded the brigade that Kilpatrick had ordered to pursue Stuart from Buckland. Davies would escape capture; many of his men were not as fortunate. (loc)

to Davies's Federal cavalrymen. Davis directed his lead regiment, the 2nd New York Cavalry, to remain where they were, while he started the remainder of his brigade back to Buckland. Unfortunately for Davies and his men, the firing around Buckland proved to be the signal for Stuart to counterattack with his division up the Warrenton Turnpike.

Putting up stiff resistance, the 2nd New York Cavalry was able to temporarily halt Stuart's advance. However, a charge by the 1st North Carolina Cavalry was soon able to brush the New Yorkers away. The New Yorkers were veteran troopers, though, and soon rallied and again were able to stop Stuart's men before being driven from their position by yet another Confederate cavalry charge. This scenario happened multiple times as Stuart's men drove Davies's men back towards Buckland.

There, Custer had his hands full with Fitz Lee. The Confederates soon dismounted enough men that Custer believed that he was facing a large infantry force. Adding to Custer's woes was the fact that his brigade had used most of their ammunition during the morning fight against Stuart and was now running dangerously low on cartridges. Believing he faced a strong enemy and with little ammunition, when the Confederates started to flank the Michigan Brigade, Custer decided that he had no choice but to re-cross Broad Run with his men. At the time, Davies's brigade was still a mile west of Buckland.

With his retreat route now blocked by Confederates, Davies was in a danger of being surrounded and his entire brigade captured. The only way to save a majority of his men, he decided, was to have them cut cross country north towards Thoroughfare Gap. In order to gain time to save his wagons, Davies ordered the 1st West Virginia Cavalry to join the 2nd New York Cavalry fighting Stuart while the 5th New York Cavalry was sent to hold back Fitz Lee's men.

Davies's men were successful in initially blunting the Confederate attack, though the overwhelming Confederate numbers soon proved to be decisive. The Federals soon began to fall back, quickly turning into a rout, with unit cohesion destroyed. This running fight was later nicknamed the Buckland Races.

Eventually, the Confederates were even able to put Custer's men to flight. The pursuit continued until Confederate cavalrymen ran into the head of Federal infantry around Gainesville. After marching and fighting nearly all day, the Confederates were content to finally fall back towards Warrenton.

The battle of Buckland Mills, as the fighting on October 19 was later called, proved that the Confederate cavalry was still a formidable opponent. While losing approximately 50 men, the Confederates were able to inflict nearly 200 casualties on the Federals. In addition, many Federal wagons were captured, among them Custer's personal wagon containing love letters to his sweetheart. Confederate officers quickly forwarded the letters to the Richmond newspapers, which published them to the embarrassment of Custer. A Confederate soldier also penned a humorous song about the battle, again at the expense of the Federal cavalrymen.

Stuart's victory, however, did not change the strategic situation facing the Confederate army, and by the end of the month, Stuart was with the rest of Lee's army back in Central Virginia where the campaign opened with so much promise just a few weeks before.

*Early in the fight, Custer and his staff watched the battle close to the Broad Run Bridge. After a Confederate artillery shell landed in their midst, the party retreated to a safer distance. (dw)*

After retreating from Buckland earlier in the day, Stuart rallied his command on the hills around New Baltimore and counterattacked Davies' brigade. (dw)

Capt. Willard Glazier of the 2nd New York Cavalry was captured at Buckland Mills. After a previous attempt to escape from a Confederate POW camp failed, Glazier successfully escaped in 1864. (wg)

*At Buckland*

The town of Buckland was formed in 1797 on land owned by the Love family. The town quickly grew up around the mill on Broad Run and the turnpike. Since it was on one of the few turnpikes in Northern Virginia that linked Washington with central Virginia, this small town saw more than its fair share of distinguished visitors, including Washington, Jefferson, Madison, Monroe, Lafayette, and later, even Theodore Roosevelt. Today, the Buckland Preservation Society has protected much of this town for future generations. But please remember: though preserved, this land is all still private property.

The Buckland Post Office where you parked was constructed around 1800 and was originally used as a store. Facing away from the post office, to your right is the location of the Buckland Mill, built in 1790. Portions of the current building date to the original mill. The white building directly across the road from the post office is Brooke's Tavern. Built around 1790, both Monroe and Lafayette stayed there during the latter's 1825 tour of the U.S. Directly to your left is the Dr. Brown house. Built in 1855, it is visible in the Alfred Waud drawing of the battle.

As you leave Buckland, please take special care. This intersection with Route 29 is very dangerous. Use extreme caution.

To visit another interpreted portion of the Buckland battlefield, take a right onto Route 29 then a left onto Rt. 215 (Vint Hill Road). Make your immediate left into the parking lot. You will see a Civil War Trails marker to the left along with a Bristoe Station Campaign Mobile Tour marker.

**This postwar engraving of the battle of Buckland Mills illustrates the confusion of the cavalry fight.** (wg)

**The harried retreat of Union cavalrymen north along the Warrenton Turnpike and nearby hills would later be dubbed "The Buckland Races."** (pr)

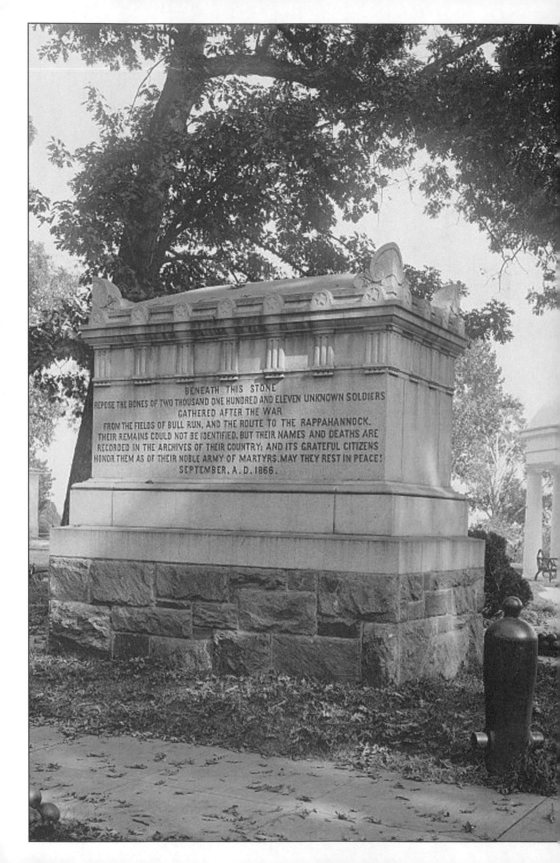

BENEATH THIS STONE
REPOSE THE BONES OF TWO THOUSAND ONE HUNDRED AND ELEVEN UNKNOWN SOLDIERS
GATHERED AFTER THE WAR
FROM THE FIELDS OF BULL RUN, AND THE ROUTE TO THE RAPPAHANNOCK.
THEIR REMAINS COULD NOT BE IDENTIFIED, BUT THEIR NAMES AND DEATHS ARE
RECORDED IN THE ARCHIVES OF THEIR COUNTRY; AND ITS GRATEFUL CITIZENS
HONOR THEM AS OF THEIR NOBLE ARMY OF MARTYRS. MAY THEY REST IN PEACE!
SEPTEMBER, A.D. 1866.

# "We Never Blushed Before"

## CONCLUSION

While the fighting at Buckland was a dramatic Confederate victory, it did not change the strategic situation facing Lee. After destroying as much of the Orange & Alexandria Railroad north of the Rappahannock River as possible, Lee retreated south of the river with most of his army. After slowing the Federal pursuit, Stuart's cavalry soon rejoined them.

With the majority of the Army of Northern Virginia safely behind the Rappahannock, Lee decided to keep a small portion of this army north of the river as a bridgehead near Rappahannock Station. Elements of Maj. Gen. Jubal Early's division manned this dangerous bulge in the Confederate line. Believing that the year's campaigning was over, Lee desired to have a bridgehead north of the Rappahannock for future operations.

Lee's efforts to delay the Federal march by destroying the railroad did slow the Federal pursuit but for not as long as he thought it would. Being forced to rebuild the railroad, Lee imagined, would delay the Federals from reaching the Rappahannock River for most of the fall. By the end of October, though, Federal engineers were able to repair the nearly 30 miles of railroad from Manassas to the Rappahannock.

With their logistical network repaired, by the beginning of November the entire Army of the Potomac was again facing Lee. The two armies stood roughly where they'd been at the start of the campaign.

**After the Civil War ended, Federal war dead in Northern Virginia, including those killed during the Bristoe campaign, were reinterred in Arlington National Cemetery. (loc)**

\*　　\*　　\*

After 1865, the Bristoe Station campaign became a small footnote in the annuals of the war. Most

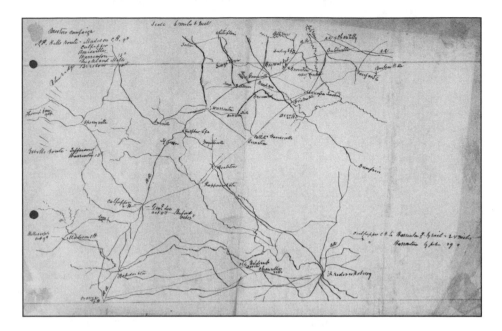

Completed at the end of the campaign, this map by David McIntosh highlights the areas of Central and Northern Virginia the armies marched through. (vh)

accounts of the Civil War in Virginia went from the aftermath of Gettysburg to Grant coming east, completely glossing over the fall campaigns. This unfortunate tendency obscures the true importance this campaign had for the outcome of the war.

While popular memory views Gettysburg as the turning point of the war, the fact remains that in October 1863 the war very well could have gone either way. While the Union war effort had scored two impressive victories at Vicksburg and Gettysburg, the protests and even riots against the Federal draft in many Northern cities in the summer of 1863 showcased how unpredictable popular support for the Lincoln administration's handling of the war could be. In Ohio and New York, conservative Democrats enjoyed popular support. The Lincoln administration nervously followed the race for the governor of Ohio, where prominent Democrat Clement Vallandigham was campaigning on the platform that the war was a failure and that the Southern states should be allowed to secede.

Besides the race in Ohio, November 1863 hosted numerous Congressional and state elections. The Union also had received a major setback with the defeat of Maj. Gen. William Rosecrans's army at Chickamauga. Had Lee's army scored another Confederate victory within weeks of Chickamauga,

it is probable that the Northern electorate would have behaved as they did a year before, electing a Democratic majority into office. With the two most populous Northern states controlled by Lincoln opponents and more Democrats in Congress, the Union war effort would have been severely curtailed, if not completely derailed.

Besides political repercussions, the Bristoe Station campaign further bloodied the two armies while they were still recovering from the summer campaign. In a 10-day period, the Army of the Potomac lost 136 men killed, 733 wounded, and 1,423 captured or missing. If the fighting at Kelly's Ford and Rappahannock Station are accounted for, the Federals lost 2,753 men in a one-month period. Likewise, the Confederates had 1,539 men killed or wounded and 2,854 captured or missing for a total of 4,393 casualties.

As a whole, the casualties suffered during the Bristoe Station campaign were twice the number of the casualties suffered during the First Manassas campaign and roughly equal to Sherman's Carolina campaign.

Besides absolute numbers, the soldiers that both armies lost were hard to replace. The Confederacy was already scraping the manpower barrel and could ill-afford to lose valuable soldiers as they had at Bristoe Station. While the Federals were able to replace many of their losses, from this moment in the war, the majority of new soldiers entering the army were substitutes or draftees,

This Alfred Waud sketch shows the Federals burning the Orange and Alexandria Railroad bridge over the Rappahannock River on October 13, 1863. As the Federals retreated northward in front of Lee, they destroyed most of the railroad bridges along the way. (vh)

lowering the overall quality of the Federal army.

Though Meade was consistently criticized that fall, he handled the Army of the Potomac with competence and was pragmatic in his reaction to Lee's movements. The Lincoln administration put great pressure on him to follow up the success of Gettysburg, but Meade was not up to the task of being an aggressive commander and proved too cautious. He did prove, though—unlike previous commanders—that he was able to handle Lee's aggressiveness. Later that winter, though, Meade fully expected to be removed from command. Lincoln had, after all, dealt with over-cautious commanders before.

As able as Meade proved to be, his corps commanders provided a mixed record during the campaign. Warren's star continued to rise—although it probably would not go any higher than it did on October 14. Of the other corps commanders, only Sedgwick and Warren would be with the Army of the Potomac by the time Lt. Gen. U. S. Grant arrived in 1864. The Bristoe and Mine Run campaigns would be the undoing of Sykes, Newton, and French.

Besides the "Buckland Races," the Federal cavalry represented themselves well. Custer proved he was a capable brigade commander, and Buford once again proved himself to be one of the elite. Unfortunately, he would not have long to live, dying in December of typhoid.

His "entrapment" at Auburn notwithstanding, Stuart handled his cavalry well in the campaign. Still smarting from southern criticism from the Gettysburg campaign, Stuart was back to his old form. The Confederate cavalry successfully screened the infantry's movement and kept Meade in the dark for most of the campaign, plus he scored several successes at Brandy Station and Buckland.

On the other hand, the conduct of Hill and Ewell was unspectacular. The departure of Longstreet left Lee a void in leadership that he could not fill. Neither commander efficiently marched their infantry. Hill proved once again, in his impatient attack at Bristoe Station, that he was brash, and Ewell again failed to be aggressive at Auburn and Bristoe. The impact of casualties on the Confederate leadership was starting to be apparent. As Jefferson Davis wrote about Hill's conduct at Bristoe Station, "There was a want of vigilance."

Lee had failed to bring about and win a decisive battle against Meade. Nor did his actions alter the strategic situation out west in Chattanooga, where Bragg was attempting to lay siege. Lee did prove, though, that although wounded after Gettysburg, the Army of Northern Virginia was not impotent. He had easily moved Meade back from the Rapidan to within 20 miles of Washington, D.C.—yet he had nothing to show for it either.

Writing a few days after the campaign ended, Maj. David McIntosh recorded a story going through the Army of Northern Virginia that best captures the result of this campaign: "General Lee's comment of the campaign, I have heard by the following quotation: 'We've grieved, we've mourned, we've wept, we never blushed before.'"

Opportunities for the Confederates to bring about a successful conclusion of the war were dwindling, and soon a new Federal commander would arrive that would bring about a new phase of the war.

Never again would Lee hold the initiative.

# *"Bury These Poor Men"* — *Lee and Hill at Bristoe Station*

## APPENDIX A

### BY BILL BACKUS

Perhaps the most famous incident from the battle of Bristoe Station was the rebuke Robert E. Lee gave to A. P. Hill after both surveyed the human wreckage after the disastrous assault. Before riding away, Lee is said to have told an embarrassed Hill, "Well, well General, bury these poor men and let us say no more about it."

While exchange is sometimes used to showcase Marse Robert's gentlemanly character, did it actually happen? There are at least five different accounts of the Lee-Hill exchange. Of the five, four were published in memoirs after the war ended.

The earliest, a contemporary version of the Lee-Hill exchange, was recorded by Captain William Seymour of the famed Louisiana Tigers. Seymour claimed in his October 15 diary entry that, while his brigade was posted nearby, he saw both Lee and Hill. "The General seemed to be in no good humor and casting a glance over the field thickly strewed with dead Confederates sharply rebuked Gen. Hill to send immediately for his pioneer corps to bury his unfortunate dead. Gen. Hill recognized a rebuke in the tone and manner of his commander and replied, 'this is my fault, General.' 'Yes,' said Lee, 'it is your fault; you committed a great blunder yesterday; your line of battle was too short, too thin, and your reserves were too far behind.' Poor Hill, he appeared deeply humiliated by this speech."

The second version of the exchange between Lee and Hill after the battle was included in an undated article about A. P. Hill written by Jedediah Hotchkiss. After arriving on the battlefield, Hotchkiss related that "Gen. Lee and staff, accompanied by Gen. Early and staff, rode up to the vicinity of the engagement, where Gen. Lee, ascertaining what had happened, reproached Gen. Hill in most bitter terms for the manner in which he had brought on this engagement, and for the horrible results that had followed, displaying a great deal of bitter feeling in what he said to Gen. Hill." (Hotchkiss made no mention of the incident, or the battle, in his famed diary.)

**Remnants of 20th century agriculture on the battlefield remain against the back drop of modern development.** (cm)

Another variant of Lee rebuking his Third Corps commander in a less-than-cordial manner appeared in William Poague's 1903 military memoir *A Gunner with Stonewall*. In his account of the Lee-Hill exchange,

Cartographer Jedadiah Hotchkiss (top) and artillerist Armistead Long (bottom) wrote two of the five known accounts of the famous Lee-Hill exchange. Hotchkiss's diary is widely recognized as a fair and credible primary source, so his account of the exchange (which did not appear in his diary), has been given much credibility over the years. Likewise, Long's one-time service on Lee's staff gave him unusual access to the commander, and so his account has similarly been given much credence. However, it seems neither man was actually present for the exchange. (loc)

Poague remembered Hill trying to explain his blunder and advocate for a resumption of the campaign. "One who was near enough to hear what passed told me that General Lee's reply was 'General Hill, I think you had better attend to the burying of your dead,' and that he was evidently not pleased with Hill's management of the affair." Poague's account is noteworthy because, instead of placing him with the generals like other authors did, Poague noted that it was an unnamed person that overheard the Lee-Hill exchange.

Perhaps the most famous version of Lee recommending Hill about burying, and then forgetting, his men appeared in Armistead Long's *Memoirs of Robert E. Lee*. Long had served on Lee's staff during the war and was in a unique position to write about Lee's wartime service. However, there are two major problems with Long's account of Lee at Bristoe. By the time Long's manuscript was published in 1886, Lee had been dead for nearly 20 years. During that time, the Lost Cause narrative had taken ahold of Southern literature of the war. That Lost Cause narrative stressed the gentlemanly portrait of Lee as the ideal Southern officer, and Long's account fit perfectly within this framework. Secondly, and perhaps most importantly, by the time the Bristoe Station campaign had started, Long was promoted from Lee's staff and placed in command of General Richard Ewell's Second Corps artillery. While Long may have indeed had the good fortune to have been close enough to Lee to hear his exchange with Hill, it's not likely that Long just happened to be near Lee instead of his command at a time when it appeared that the Confederates would renew their assault. That casts doubt upon the veracity of Long's account.

The final variation of Lee telling Hill to bury his men is found in Henry Heth's memoirs, written around 1897. According to his memoirs, Heth, Hill, and Lee were all riding over the battlefield. In Heth's account, Lee's only remark to Hill's explanation of the failed assault was "General, bury your dead." Like Long, there are problems with Heth's version of the post-battle exchange. The major problem is that no other account has Lee, Hill, and Heth together. Heth had a tendency to elevate his importance in the Army of Northern Virginia throughout his memoir, and this exchange seems to be yet another instance of Heth attempting to improve his postwar reputation. Since Heth's memoirs were written after Long's book, it appears that Heth used Long's

account as a basis for his recollection. (Heth's memoirs remained unpublished until 1974.)

With five different versions of the Lee-Hill exchange, how can we make sense of it? While we will probably never be able to reconstruct the exchange with total accuracy, it is more than likely that Lee reacted to Hill similar to the account that appears in Seymour's account. Not only is it more contemporary than the other accounts, but from other events during the war, historians know that Lee had a habit of berating his staff and generals during times of great stress. Soldiers near the generals quickly spread the exchange, as stated by Poague, so that Lee's rebuke of Hill was probably well known within the Army of Northern Virginia by the end of the Bristoe campaign. After the war, authors such as Long and Heth edited the exchange to project a more gentlemanly image of Lee, one that we still have today.

Regardless of the exact phrase that Lee used, Hill indeed buried his men, many of whom are still buried at Bristoe Station today.

The Bristoe Station Battlefield Heritage Park visitor center peeks above the hilltop where the Lee-Hill exchange took place. (cm)

# The Adventure-filled Reconnaissance of the 1st Maine Cavalry

## APPENDIX B

## BY JOHN R. TOLE

October 12, 1864, proved to be a critical day in the Bristoe campaign. Union Maj. Gen. George Meade desperately needed answers to two vital questions: Where was Confederate Gen. Robert E. Lee and what were his intentions?

Col. J. Irwin Gregg's 2nd Cavalry Brigade, operating from its base at Warrenton Sulpher Springs on the Rappahannock River, was assigned to provide early warning of any attempt by Lee to cross the upper river fords and cut off Meade's line of communications with Washington. Gregg held much of the brigade near its camp to scout along the river above and below the Springs. Early on the morning of the 12th, Gregg directed Col. Charles. H. Smith and the 1st Maine Cavalry to reconnoiter near the Blue Ridge in order to detect any enemy movements in that vicinity or in the gaps of the mountains.

Little did Smith's men know that they were embarking on a circuitous and exhausting 36-hour adventure.

The 1st Maine left Sulpher Springs before daybreak and headed directly west for Gaines Crossroads (modern-day Ben Venue), where the Richmond Road from Culpeper led northward to Chester Gap. As they proceeded, they caught glimpses of small groups

**One of the most scenic villages in Virginia, Washington, or "Little Washington," now has fewer people living in the town than it did during the Civil War. The Rappahannock County Courthouse, built in 1834, was designed by a student of Thomas Jefferson.** (ro)

**Today boasting some of the best-preserved slave dwellings in the South, Ben Venue was a large plantation that played witness to the 1st Maine Cavalry on their reconnaissance.** (jt)

of horsemen, possibly Confederate cavalry or Mosby's Rangers, but none interfered with their progress. At the crossroads, Smith left Company I under Capt. Paul Chadbourne and headed farther westward another 5 miles to Little Washington, leaving another small observation party midway between the two points.

At the same time, probably about midday, Lt. William Harris of Company F, escorted by 12 men, was sent back to the Sulpher Springs with an interim report indicating—ironically, as it would turn out—that, thus far, no Rebel activity was observed. They passed quietly through Amissville, but as they headed for the Springs, they discovered a cavalry fight in progress at the village of Jeffersonton, several miles west of the Rappahannock. Pennsylvanians and New Yorker's from Gregg's brigade were engaged with the 11th and 12th Virginia cavalry. (While Lt. Gen. Richard Ewell's corps, and Lee himself, were not far behind the Southern cavalry, there is no indication that Harris's party realized this.)

His path blocked, Harris reversed direction toward Amissville. There, he received a much larger surprise. Where his route was clear hours earlier, he now found the lead elements of Lt.

Gen. A. P. Hill's Confederate corps just arriving at the village. Harris stumbled onto exactly the intelligence that Meade needed, but he and his comrades were now caught between the two Confederate forces. Harris abandoned his horses and equipment, captured several prisoners, marched through the Rebel camp, and set out cross-country.

Arriving at New Baltimore, Harris narrowly avoided capture by Mosby's Rangers—but later, he was not so lucky as elements of Col. Elijah White's 35th Virginia Cavalry apprehended him and his men. White's men took the captives into the mountains for several days and thence to Sulpher Springs—ironically, Harris's originally intended destination—which was now in Confederate control. There, he eventually escaped. Timing being everything, however, Harris's critical knowledge of Lee's location and movements would obviously go for naught.

Meanwhile, when Smith and his force arrived at Little Washington, 100 troopers under Lt. Col. Stephen Boothby and Maj. George Brown were directed to continue five miles farther west to Sperryville, the gateway to Thornton Gap—the next major Blue Ridge crossing south of Chester Gap. Shortly before sunset, this detachment returned to Little Washington and reported no activity near the mountains.

After an hour's rest, the entire command headed eastward back to Gaines Crossroads, picking up the intermediate scouts on the way. At the crossroads, Capt. Chadbourne and his men were sent ahead of the main column to Sulpher Springs with a (second) report of no observed Rebel movements. However when Chadbourne neared Amissville, he was fired upon and quickly reported to Smith that a large force was in his front. Inquiries among local residents indicated that Hill's corps had arrived at the village since about 3 p.m.

Suddenly, Smith had the information he was tasked to find: Hill's location. But as with Harris, he knew he was unable to deliver this knowledge to Sulpher Springs as a Confederate corps now blocked his path (actually two corps blocked him, but, at the time, Smith had no way of knowing Ewell's position near the Springs). To deliver his news, Smith would have to give Hill a wide berth if capture was to be avoided.

This Alfred Waud drawing depicts the 1st Maine cavalry skirmishing in the field. As depicted in the sketch, much of the fighting by cavalry was done dismounted. (loc)

In preparation for a possible attack, Smith formed his two lead companies into a skirmish line facing Amissville. He ordered the remainder of the regiment to countermarch to Gaines Crossroads, with the skirmishers bringing up the rear. To slow possible pursuit, he burned a bridge over a small stream—likely the eastern branch of Battle Run, approximately one mile east of the crossroads.

When he arrived there, Smith learned that Boothby located a 14-year-old black boy who "knows the way most thar" to Orleans, a village northeast of Amissville on the eastern side of the Rappahannock River. About midnight, with the boy in the lead, the column set off to find a safe crossing of the river well above Amissville. In his official report, Col. Gregg indicated the route taken included Keysville, a small intersection several miles north of Gaines Crossroads. Just east of Keysville is Rock Ford on the Rappahannock, a crossing that would allow an undiscovered approach to Orleans from the northwest.

Once across the river, their young guide soon reached the limit of his known world and was sent on his way. Soon thereafter, the troopers came to the home of a middle-aged Southerner who, enticed with a small bribe, agreed to guide them on to Orleans. When they reached the village, their second guide was dismissed.

Below Orleans, Smith and his men turned onto the Warrenton Turnpike hoping to encounter Union pickets outside the town. As they neared

Warrenton at about 3 a.m., a camp of sleeping cavalry was discovered beside the pike. Without orders, Maj. Sidney Thaxter rode into the camp and loudly cried, "What regiment is this?" to which he received a lethargic yet indignant reply: "The Twelfth Virginia, you damned fool!"

Fortunately, Thaxter was able to return unscathed. He reported that the camp was virtually silent with not even a guard on duty. Smith later indicated that it would have been possible to capture the entire regiment of Southern horsemen but, remembering his mission, he chose instead to push on so as to reach Meade as quickly as possible.

But which way to go? While there was no pursuit by the Southerners, the path of the 1st Maine was once again blocked.

Smith led his men off to the northwest in the direction of New Baltimore on a course he believed to be roughly parallel to the Warrenton Pike. After travelling several miles by dead reckoning, the regiment came upon a plantation house where they awakened the owner and his young black servant. The owner informed them that they were about a mile from the Warrenton-New Baltimore Turnpike, which would take them to the latter place from the northwest. Taking the boy as their third guide of the night, they pressed on, reaching New Baltimore about sunrise.

After a brief rest, Smith directed the regiment on to Bristoe Station and dispatched Major Brown to bring the information on Hill's location to Meade, a task finally accomplished about midday on Oct 13. By then, with reports of the previous day's fighting at Sulpher Springs and Jeffersonton and the sighting of Confederate infantry there, Meade realized that Lee was indeed attempting to outflank the Army of the Potomac. The "old goggled-eyed snapping turtle" had his army in full retreat northward along the Orange and Alexandria Railroad tracks. The 1st Maine's intelligence on Hill's movements, collected with such heroic effort, helpful though it might have been, was by now old news.

The 1st Maine travelled nearly 100 miles in 36 hours by the time they reached Bristoe. In their effort to locate Lee's maneuver, they had, ironically, performed the widest flanking movement of the entire campaign. After resting for almost a day, they watched on the afternoon of October 14 from well beyond the eastern side of the railroad embankment near Bristoe Station as Hill attacked and was repulsed by Warren's column.

Years later, members of the 1st Maine would view this reconnaissance as one of their most important activities in the war. At a reunion in 1883, in an apparent instance of misremembering, Col. Smith repeatedly indicated that his force had gone as far as Chester Gap during their patrol. However, given other elements of the story, it is virtually certain that he should have referred instead to Gaines Crossroads.

In a sad footnote, Lt. Harris, who missed the opportunity to provide the earliest information on Hill's whereabouts to Meade, was found near the unit's camp on the Chickahominy River in May 1864 with a gunshot to the head, an apparent suicide.

JOHN R. TOLE *is an MIT-trained engineer, local historian, author, and musician performing both period (Civil War, Colonial, and 1800s) as well as more modern acoustic tunes. He is president of the Rappahannock Historical Society and is writing a book on Rappahannock County in the Civil War.*

# *"Miserable, Miserable Management": The Battles of Rappahannock Station and Kelly's Ford*

## APPENDIX C
### BY MICHAEL BLOCK

After the culmination of the Bristoe campaign, Confederate Gen. Robert E. Lee moved his army south through Fauquier County. In doing so, the Confederates destroyed the Orange & Alexandria (O&A) Railroad and stripped the railroad of its rail iron. By October 26, 1863, Lee's army removed the last accessible iron from the Bealeton area. As the heavily laden wagons moved south towards the Rappahannock River, the Stonewall Brigade protected its precious cargo from Federal cavalry.

Both Lee and Army of the Potomac's commander, Gen. George G. Meade, settled in—Lee behind the Rappahannock River in Culpeper County and Meade in Fauquier County. Lee placed Ewell's and Hill's corps along the river, guarding the river fords. The cavalry monitored the flanks. Anticipating no more fighting until spring, both armies began building winter quarters.

The modern railroad bridge across the Rappahannock River sits in the same location as the wartime bridge. In this area, the Confederates on the left bank of the river had to swim to the right bank to safety or surrender. (ro)

Military and civilian leadership in Washington had other ideas.

By November 1, railroad engineers rebuilt the O&A to Warrenton Junction. Meade had concerns that a single line wasn't sufficient to supply his army, and requested a "change of base" to the Fredericksburg area. This was rejected, fearing a repeat of events from the previous December when Lee punished Burnside for entering the city. Instead,

**Here Upton's Federals broke through Brig. Gen. Robert Hoke's line of North Carolinians. The Rappahannock River and pontoon bridge crossing is in the tree line in the center of the photograph. (ro)**

Meade was directed to press Lee. Ordered not to go to his left, and with roads to his right marginal, Meade's sole option was down the O&A toward Rappahannock Station.

South of the river, Lee still looked for an opportunity to strike. He positioned his army to protect the fords, and manned a tete de pont with a brigade of infantry at Rappahannock Station. This position was originally built in 1862, protecting the railroad bridge site and, depending on ownership, could be reconfigured facing either north or south. Lee hoped to use the position "to threaten any flank movement the enemy might make above or below, and thus compel him to divide his forces."

On November 6, Maj. Gen. Jubal Early's Louisiana Infantry Brigade under Brig. Gen. Harry Hays filed into the Rappahannock Station rifle-pits and two forts, relieving Walker's brigade, of Maj. Gen. Edward Johnson's division. Joining them was the four-gun Louisiana Artillery.

Near Kelly's Ford, the 2nd North Carolina Infantry Regiment guarded the fords, stretching over two miles, with just 322 men. Complicating the situation, the ground in Fauquier County was higher and thus dominated Culpeper County.

That evening, Meade issued orders to advance. Maj. General John Sedgwick's VI Corps would move to Rappahannock Station, supported by elements of the V Corps. Sedgwick commanded the right column. The left column would be led by Maj. Gen. William French, who controlled his own III Corps, as well as the I and II corps. French's objective was to move against and cross at Kelly's Ford. Movement began at daybreak, November 7.

The weather that Saturday was clear and brisk, with a very strong wind coming from the South. As the Federals marched toward contact, soldiers sang and discarded playing cards and other items that they did not want found on their bodies were they to be shot. By 11 a.m., both columns were approaching their objectives.

Sedgwick's corps advanced generally along the Culpeper-Warrenton road. French advanced to Morrisville, and then towards Kelly's Ford. Sykes's corps was charged with protecting the ground between the two columns. A 900-man skirmish brigade was formed from the 1st and 2nd Divisions to "seal" the ground between the O&A and the Rappahannock.

French would use his III Corps to carry Kelly's Ford, with the II Corps supporting. The I Corps remained back, protecting the pontoon and supply trains.

Confederate pickets observed and reported the Federal arrival. At Kelly's Ford, the 1st U.S. Sharpshooters pushed the North Carolinians back across the river. Upriver, the Louisianans withdrew as Sedgwick's men approached. Sykes's men did not face any real opposition, linking with Sedgwick's left, and securing their right on the Rappahannock, denying the Rebels any chance of escaping downriver.

Both Sedgwick and French had overpowering artillery. French placed two batteries on the Mount Holly Church ridge and another above the Rappahannock Station-Kelly's Ford road. A single battery protected the Tar Heels.

Sedgwick deployed six artillery batteries on ridges north and northeast of the Confederate forts. Because of the Federal artillery placement, it was difficult for the Louisiana battery and the two Virginia batteries on the hills south of the river to respond effectively. "[T]he fire from these batteries crossed," Early wrote in his report, "and in a great measure enfiladed our position and rendered the brigade quite unsafe." Lee also saw the futility of his batteries across the river providing counter-battery fire and ordered them to cease firing.

At Kelly's Ford, Capt. W. D. Vachet of the 20th Indiana described the advance across the river. "The ball now opened rather briskly," he wrote.

Drawn by Waud on October 13, 1863, this sketch shows the Federal defenses at Rapahannock Station protecting the Rappahannock railroad bridge facing south. When the Confederates occupied these earthworks in November, they did little work to reface them towards the north. (loc)

This Alfred Waud sketch shows the Federal infantry crossing the Rappahannock River and assaulting the Confederate position at Kelly's Ford on November 7. (loc)

We pushed their front line through and over the river, when they took refuge in their rifle pits just on the other side. Gen. [Hobart] Ward decided to make short work of it, and he ordered the sharpshooters, 20th Indiana and 40th New York to go over the river on the double quick and take these works. Away they went, with one of their unearthly yells. You can image the boys going through the river nearly waist deep, old Hobart Ward on his white horse at the head of them . . . we soon had them in a tight place. We took 480 prisoners . . . and drove the others flying right over the open plain to the woods. The loss in this skirmish was 10 killed and 60 wounded in our division, and not a gun was fired by any other troops.

The 30th North Carolina, supporting the

2nd North Carolina, was never able to get into position. Nonetheless, Maj. Gen. Robert Rodes wrote afterwards, "The Second North Carolina behaved very handsomely." Rodes explained

> [t]he loss of prisoners in this regiment resulted in Lt. Col. Stallings holding his regiment in position in order to save the 30th, which had come to his relief on his left. The 30th North Carolina, was speedily broken and demoralized under the concentrated artillery fire which swept the ground over which it march[ed]....it arrived at the mill in great confusion and became uncontrollable. Many of the men refused utterly to leave the shelter of the houses when ordered to fall back. All who refused were of course captured.

Rodes reported that he lost 309 men in this "skirmish." By nightfall, two pontoon bridges lay across Kelly's Ford.

It would not go well for the Confederates at Rappahannock Station, either. Hays was reinforced by Brig. Gen. Robert Hoke's three North Carolina infantry regiments, under Col. Archibald Godwin, who double-timed from camp and entered the works after 4 p.m. Hays arrived and assumed command.

At 5 o'clock, Sedgwick realized that time was at hand. He ordered Brig. Gen. David Russell to advance his division and carry the works. Russell ordered the brigades of Col. Peter Ellmaker and Col. Emory Upton forward.

Ellmaker's 6th Maine and 5th Wisconsin led the assault. "At about dusk," a Mainer recounted, "Gen. Russell gave the command for the [6th Maine], then deployed as a double line of skirmishers, to assault the works of the enemy . . . and he joined in the charge himself."

One of the first into the works was Sgt. Otis Roberts of the 6th Maine. Entering the works, Roberts realized that he was surrounded, and he called out his surrender. As the rest of the command came up, Maj. George Fuller of the 6th Maine wrote of what happened next: "Roberts . . . with only five men, rushed upon the color-bearer of the 8th Louisiana Regiment, who was in the midst of his color company, and after a hand-to-hand conflict, in which the bayonet was freely used, succeeded in capturing the colors, compelling the whole company to surrender." Roberts won the Medal of Honor, one of three awarded that day.

The two regiments were joined by the remainder of the brigade, and 80 men from the 20th Maine, whom, as part of the V Corps skirmish line, saw the 6th Maine go into the works and followed. On the right, Upton—commanding a brigade for the first time—used two regiments to assault the right.

"Under cover of darkness we formed within 100 yards of their works," Upton wrote. "I told the 5th Maine that the troops from Maine had won laurels on every field, and that the gallant 5th must not be behind them. A few words to the 121st New York sufficed to rouse their determination to the highest pitch."

Frank Morris, Upton's aide-de-camp, described the assault:

> We dashed up the threatening line of works regardless of the storm of balls that passed through us, pressed on, and were soon at the top, and then in possession. It was quite dark, and the enemy could not see the smallness of our numbers. At this point, Upton, in a voice loud enough to be heard by the enemy, cried. "The first line will lie down when fired on, as there are three others to support them." In fact we had but one small line of battle; but the enemy hearing this, and thinking themselves out numbered and overpowered when we made a vigorous charge on them, surrendered at discretion.

The 6th North Carolina had been issued 1,000 rounds of ammunition on October 22. That was quickly depleted. The Tar Heels began to fight with swords, bayonets, clubbed muskets, and bare hands. A few soldiers would manage to fight their way across the pontoon bridge under a hail of enemy bullets. Other soldiers attempted to swim the river; however, most were forced to return due to the severe cold and swiftness of the deep water.

The Louisianans, cut off from the pontoon bridge and with a deep river in their rear, fought desperately. Muskets were seized and torn from

This Alfred Waud engraving shows the brigade of Col. Emory Upton piercing the Confederate line held by Brig. Gen. Robert Hoke's North Carolinians. The pontoon bridge across the Rappahannock River can be seen in the background. (loc)

From this hill top, Federal infantry under Col. Emory Upton launched their assault on the Confederate bridgehead at Rappahannock Station (in the tree line). (dw)

the grasp of those who held them, and men grappled and fought with their fists. Inside the large redoubt, the melee was frightful. The Rebel artillerymen stuck to their guns, fighting savagely with rammers, hand-spikes, swords, or whatever was at hand.

As darkness enveloped the battlefield, the Yankees took control of the bridge, isolating the remaining Rebels. The Confederates, not knowing the true strength of the attacking force, but knowing

**Alfred Waud sketched this image the day after the battle of Rappahannock Station, showing the redoubts of Hay's Louisianans. In the foreground, Federal soldiers hold captured Confederate battle flags.** (loc)

their line was penetrated, began surrendering.

The Confederate suffered nearly 1,700 casualties—1,590 in prisoners—lost the Louisiana Battery, 2,000 stand of arms, a pontoon bridge and seven battle flags. Ellmaker's and Upton's brigades lost 69 killed, 256 wounded, and 1 missing.

Lee and Early departed the river just as the Federal assault began. Darkness and a strong wind from the south denied them sight or sound of the fighting. Neither realized what transpired.

"The enemy advanced upon us at Kelly's Ford and at Rappahannock Station," recapped Maj. Walter Taylor, Lee's adjutant,

> "effected a crossing at the former place and rushed upon our men who were at the latter place defending the bridge, overwhelmed and captured most of them. Thus in a very few words I tell you the saddest chapter in the history of this army. There were captured about 12 or 1500 men and a battery of artillery. Miserable, miserable, miserable management. . . . We are now on the outposts and this is not exactly the place for the General Commanding. No sleep tonight and tomorrow. . . ."

**MICHAEL BLOCK, a retired Air Force Intelligence Analyst, currently works for Booz Allen Hamilton. He is the vice-president of the Friends of Cedar Mountain Battlefield and is currently gathering material for a book-length study of Rappahannock Station.**

The battle forced Lee below the Rapidan River. Meade's men occupied Confederate camps, establishing winter quarters. It would be from Culpeper, and not Fauquier County, that the Overland Campaign would commence.

Many of the roads used by both armies in 1863 remain in similar condition today. This road was taken by A. P. Hill's Corps on its way to Amissville. (ro)

# "A Handsome Little Fight": The First Battle at Bristoe Station

## APPENDIX D

## BY JAY GREEVY

October 1863 was not the first time that war visited Bristoe Station. The previous summer, in the days before the Confederate victory at Second Manassas, Maj. Gen. Joseph Hooker's division moved to dislodge three brigades under Maj. Gen. Richard Ewell from the ground around the station. The brief fight that ensued along the Orange and Alexandria (O&A) Railroad, just north of a stream called Kettle Run, heavily bled regiments of both sides. The Peninsula campaign of the preceding months and the battle of Second Manassas that immediately followed the action have largely overshadowed the battle of Kettle Run (or the first battle of Bristoe Station) in history.

The first engagement at Bristoe Station came amid months of almost continuous battles and maneuvers in the spring and summer of 1862. By mid-August, following the Union Army of the Potomac's abortive Peninsula campaign, operations shifted away from Richmond. Gen. Robert E. Lee's Army of Northern Virginia and Maj. Gen. John Pope's Army of Virginia faced each other along the Rappahannock River. Lee sought to overcome Pope's army before the troops returning from Maj. Gen. George McClellan's Peninsula campaign fully reinforced it. He sent Maj. Gen. Thomas "Stonewall" Jackson on an audacious march around the Union right flank to draw Pope

The first battle of Bristoe, better known as the battle of Kettle Run, remains largely forgotten in the wider context of the Second Manassas campaign. Today, the battlefield is preserved in the Bristoe Station Battlefield Heritage Park. (cm)

back from his defenses, a rapid maneuver that began on the morning of August 25. On August 26, Jackson received reports that the O&A, Pope's vital avenue of supply, was lightly guarded several miles south of Manassas Junction at a stop called Bristoe Station. He resolved to cut the line there.

Shortly before sunset, Confederate cavalry charged east along the Brentsville Road and overran the Union outpost at the station. Jackson's infantry followed closely behind, just as a Union train was

**This wartime engraving of Maj. Gen. Joseph Hooker at Kettle Run is the only period drawing of the battle, although it is highly inaccurate. Hooker did not lead men into battle but rather provided reconnaissance—a major cause of the bungled Federal attack.** (ml)

returning from a run to Warrenton Junction. The Confederates fired on the train and attempted to derail it by placing obstacles on the tracks, but it plowed through the impediments and continued on to Manassas Junction. The engineer sounded the alarm that Rebels were present at Bristoe.

Jackson's wing achieved the initial purpose of its arduous march of the previous two days. As the Confederate column poured into Bristoe Station, they rounded up a handful of Union prisoners and switched the track to derail any subsequent trains. As darkness fell over the small cluster of buildings around the station, the Confederates heard the approach of a second Federal train from Warrenton Junction. It was greeted with musketry and careened off of the railroad after running out of track. A third met a similar end, plowing headlong into the rear of its predecessor. Soon, another locomotive approached, but it paused south of the station. The engineer, perhaps alerted by survivors from the two wrecks, threw it into reverse when bullets zipped past him. Picking up speed, the train outran its pursuers southwest to Warrenton Junction.

With Jackson's presence detected, his men wasted little time in wreaking havoc. They burned the two wrecked trains and tore up track to further inhibit the O&A's use by the Federals. The telegraph line that ran along the railroad was also cut, but not before a message from Manassas Junction reached Pope's headquarters in Warrenton Junction. It carried urgent intelligence that the engineer of the train that escaped south from Bristoe corroborated: The Confederates were in the rear of Pope's army and astride his supply line.

Late on the night of August 26, Jackson permitted his exhausted men a few hours' rest. But he pushed two regiments north to Manassas Junction, where they overwhelmed the Federal defenders and captured a bountiful supply depot. Jackson marched there early the next morning, leaving Maj. Gen. Richard Ewell's division at Bristoe as a rearguard.

The Federals, too, were active throughout the night. Union commanders prepared to dispatch troops toward Bristoe and Manassas from multiple directions to assess and counter the Confederate incursions. The first regiment called on to reconnoiter Bristoe from Warrenton Junction was the 72nd New York Infantry. It was one of five New York regiments that composed the

View of the Kettle Run battlefield from the position of Col. Henry Forno's Louisiana Brigade. The Orange and Alexandria Railroad ran through the far treeline. (ro)

After the Second Manassas Campaign, the debris from the destroyed trains at Bristoe Station were brought to Alexandria for reuse. In addition to the two trains destroyed by Jackson's men, Pope had numerous supply trains destroyed during his retreat to Fairfax. (loc)

"Excelsior Brigade" of Joseph Hooker's division, a 3rd Corps division that suffered severely at the battle of Williamsburg and other clashes during the campaign on Richmond. Hooker's veterans had little opportunity to rest and refit after the Peninsula campaign. Shipped to Alexandria to support Pope, the command was then transported to Warrenton Junction by train along the O&A. They passed Bristoe Station on their way, some units just hours before the Confederates captured it on the evening of August 26. Now the men of the 72nd New York were ordered back up the railroad.

As the 72nd neared Bristoe in the predawn hours, the formidable strength of the Confederate force there became evident. Confederate columns, illuminated by the flames from the two smoldering trains, were moving to cut them off. The 72nd's commanding officer recognized the perilous situation, and the men re-boarded the train, escaping south just as Confederate artillery began to fire on the locomotive.

At daylight, Ewell deployed the brigades of Jubal Early's Virginians, Henry Forno's Louisianans, and A. R. Lawton's Georgians on the heights around Bristoe, supported by batteries of artillery. A substantial force was needed to expel them. That task fell to "Fighting Joe" Hooker's division.

After receiving their orders before dawn,

Hooker's Federals set out around 6:00 a.m., stopping at Warrenton Junction briefly before continuing on along the railroad to Bristoe. The division was ill prepared for battle. Months of hard campaigning had depleted their numbers substantially. Each man carried 40 rounds of ammunition, which would soon prove inadequate. Most officers made the march dismounted, their horses remaining at Alexandria. As temperatures neared 90 degrees that afternoon, hundreds of stragglers fell out during their march of more than 10 miles. But the division pressed on.

By midafternoon, Confederates observed signs of the Union advance. The 6th and 8th Louisiana pulled back from their positions along Kettle Run, tearing up track and destroying the railroad bridge over the stream as they withdrew. Hooker's men sloshed through Kettle Run and deployed into line of battle. As the New York and New Jersey men of the lead brigade moved toward Bristoe on either side of the railroad, fields of high clover, short pines, and scrub brush impeded their advance. The 2nd New York and 8th New Jersey filtered through thick woods and into a large field, advancing toward a tree line on the opposite side. There the Louisianans awaited them.

When the 8th New Jersey and the 2nd New York came well within musket range, the Louisiana "Tigers" poured a volley into them. The Federals halted and returned fire, driving the Rebels that ventured into the clearing into the cover of the woods. Confederate batteries on the heights around Bristoe pounded the bluecoats with their guns. "We could see the shot and shell plough through their crowded ranks and make long lanes, and we shouted with joy," one Confederate artilleryman reminisced.

Col. Nelson Taylor quickly led three regiments of his Excelsior Brigade into the fight, tying in on the right of the 8th New Jersey, which found some relief from the withering fusillade in a ravine. The 71st, 73rd, and 74th New York, all greatly reduced in strength by recent battles and the day's march, shot their muskets into the trees before them. The battle escalated in intensity as five Union regiments in the field exchanged fire with the 6th and 8th Louisiana, later supported by the 5th Louisiana.

The exposed nature of the Federals' position was not lost on Confederate officers. The 60th

Georgia extended the line of the Louisianans on the other side of the railroad. Without a Union presence in their immediate front, they wheeled right to take up a position along the railroad embankment and poured a vicious enfilading fire into the Union flank. Dozens of Federal officers were shot down, and the 2nd New York abandoned its position and pulled back to the woods.

To confront the threat to the Union line, Taylor hurried the unengaged 70th and 72nd New York to within close range of the railroad, where the two regiments created a right angle with the rest of the battle line, providing their beleaguered comrades some relief. A brutal close-range fight between the New Yorkers and Georgians commenced. "Our comrades fell thick and fast," an officer of the 70th recalled after the battle. "All felt sad when the gallant Lt. Hoxie fell with a Minie ball through the groin." Eventually two other Union regiments arrived on the Georgians' flank, and the Confederates retreated with heavy losses as the Federals seized the railroad.

By evening, the efforts of Federal infantry to outflank the Confederates became plain, and Union artillery at last joined the battle and concentrated effective fire on the enemy positions. To his relief, Ewell received orders from Jackson to fall back if hard pressed. He pulled his brigades and artillery across Broad Run, where they reformed to counter a Union pursuit that never materialized. His regiments exhausted, shot up, and low on ammunition, Hooker kept his men south of the creek. The opposing batteries dueled in the fading light, and Confederate engineers burned the bridge over Broad Run around 6:00 p.m., ending the battle. The Confederates marched north to join Jackson later that night.

In little more than one hour of battle and the sporadic skirmishing that followed, the two Union brigades engaged lost between 300 and 330 men. Ewell's division suffered 176 casualties. Although the coming days' carnage would eclipse these losses, the afternoon of August 27 was among the costliest of the war for several regiments. The 2nd New York lost 70 men at Bristoe, more than in any other battle during the course of its service. The Fire Zouaves of the 73rd New York began the fight with only 107 men and half became casualties.

Ewell's division fought in the coming battles,

Including at Groveton on August 28, where Ewell received a bullet that cost him his leg. On August 27, however, he had managed a classic rearguard action, keeping his foe at bay without committing more than a fraction of his force to the fight. This enabled Jackson to move according to his schedule rather than at the behest of his Federal pursuers.

With the Louisianans in the distant tree line, this field is where the 2nd New York and Excelsior Brigade took heavy casualties. The distant communications tower is the location of Bristoe Station. (ro)

The convergence of Federal forces would develop a new urgency after Kettle Run, an urgency that may have later diverted the Union commander's attention from the larger strategic picture. Arriving on the field in the waning stages of the fight, Pope was emboldened by the Confederate retreat. At 9:00 p.m., he sent orders to his subordinates to hasten to Bristoe and Manassas Junction. "We shall bag the whole crowd," Pope confidently noted, believing that he could crush Jackson's command while it was divided from the rest of the army. This mentality clouded his thinking in the coming days and distracted him from the movements of the other half of Lee's force.

For several days, newspapers reported on the fight near Kettle Run with interest. The Richmond Dispatch praised Ewell for his performance in the "handsome little fight," while the *New York*

*Herald* cast the orderly Confederate withdrawal as a rout. Yet the coverage soon gave way to columns on the second battle of Manassas as the scale and outcome of that engagement became clear. With the battle of Antietam just three weeks later, the fight at Bristoe Station receded from public eye for North and South alike.

JAY GREEVY *is a native of Northern Virginia, where he has led tours of both Bristoe Station battles. He received a master's degree in American History from George Mason University and currently volunteers at Bristoe Station Battlefield Heritage Park.*

The river crossing at Hill's Mills where A. P. Hill's corps crossed the Hazel and Thornton Rivers. (cm)

# Remembering the Fall of '63

## APPENDIX E

### BY CHRIS MACKOWSKI

Here's how the general histories of the Civil War usually tell it: After the two armies fought a terrible battle in Gettysburg, the Confederates slipped away; the following spring, Ulysses S. Grant took command of the Union army, and two armies fought again in the Wilderness.

Some of those histories might toss a bone to the Western Theater and mention the battle of Chickamauga, but otherwise, all was quiet. It's as though, magically, nothing happened in the east—just a big, historical vacuum.

Ironically, the Army of Northern Virginia and the Army of the Potomac engaged in contact virtually every day in those late months of summer and throughout the fall of 1863. A cavalry clash here, a reconnaissance there. A skirmish here, a maneuver and out-maneuver there, there, and there.

There was no big, all-out, knock-down, drag-out battle, though—and that's what Abraham Lincoln needed. That's what the Northern public wanted. That's what fans of history pay attention to and remember.

Little wonder, then, that the fall campaign remains the least remembered and least studied phase of the war in the east.

"We're trapped between the two 'Gs,'" Rob Orrison tells me one afternoon. "Gettysburg and Grant. Both of them were so huge, so people pay attention to them. We get lost between that."

By "we," Rob means "Bristoe Station." He's one of the caretakers of the battlefield and the story of the battle, so it's no wonder he uses the first-person pronoun. He feels it personally.

By "we," he could also be referring not only to Bristoe Station but the other actions in the fall of 1863. The best-known are Rappahannock Station and Mine Run—but that's like saying "the best known" minor league baseball player or "the best known" Gilded Age president. Hard-cores know, but few others have an inkling.

Bristoe, Rappahannock, and Mine Run amassed a total of 5,965 casualties between them—2,231 Union and 3,734 Confederate. You could add to that list locations like Auburn, Buckland Mills, Brandy Station, Kelly's Ford, and Payne's Farm and the casualty numbers begin to swell more—not to mention all the killed, wounded, missing, and captured from the daily friction between the two armies as they probed and maneuvered. The

Like this old road trace running up from Mine Run, remnants from the fall '63 campaigns still dot the landscape. Much of the story, however, has vanished along with the physical evidence. (cm)

daily business of being on the front lines of the war was inglorious but often deadly work.

If it lacks the drama of a sweeping battle—and the correspondingly high body counts—remember that no mother, wife, or child wants to get a telegram from the War Department, no matter the reason, no matter how large or small the engagement.

To skip the fall of 1863 because it lacks a major battle is to overlook the many other opportunities and lessons it offer us.

Both commanders, for instance, found themselves hamstrung, dealing with new realities that completely worked against their strengths. Both men had well-earned reputations for aggressiveness, yet neither could strike as they wished. The back-to-back bleed-outs of Chancellorsville and Gettysburg had weakened Lee's army so badly that he lacked the physical or logistical ability to mount a credible offensive, at least in the style he was accustomed to.

The Alabama Cemetery today is only marked with a few field headstones, the remaining graves only identified by depressions in the ground. (cm)

He was also still trying to learn to use his army. Two of his top three subordinates, Lieutenant Generals Richard Ewell and A. P. Hill, had performed poorly at Gettysburg, and Lee had yet to figure out how to get them to live up to the potential he'd originally seen in them.

Lee might have benefitted from the advice and example of his other top subordinate, Lt. Gen. James Longstreet, but Richmond had temporarily transferred Longstreet to the Western Theater. For the first time, Lee had to figure out how to operate his army without the balancing eye of his Old Warhorse—a skill that would take on a new urgency after May 6, 1864, when Longstreet would be taken off the chessboard during the battle of the Wilderness. Lee would go on to suffer from an acute leadership crisis as the '64 Overland Campaign unfolded. The fall of 1863 offers a full preview.

I think of the human element at play in that leadership situation, too. Hill hailed from Culpeper and Ewell from outside Manassas. In the fall of '63, the armies traipsed through both areas. Here these men hailed from, and here they tried to come of age as lieutenant generals and corps commanders.

On the Federal side, Meade likewise found his aggressiveness blunted. The Army of the Potomac was a political beast beyond his imaginings, and Meade was up to his eyeballs. Aside from the meddling-as-usual atmosphere the army always operated in, Meade found himself besieged on a personal level as malcontent subordinates like Dan Sickles hammered him relentlessly. Meade could hardly give his full attention to command—although he tried—while he constantly had to worry about his back.

Even when he won, Meade couldn't win. After his victory at Rappahannock Station in November, he went to Washington, expecting to be congratulated. Instead, Lincoln and Secretary of War Stanton rebuffed him, and his immediate supervisor, General in Chief Henry Halleck, scolded rather than praised him. Rappahannock Station, after all, wasn't "the big win."

That makes Meade's refusal to launch an all-out attack at Mine Run in late November all the more astounding— and that phase of the campaign all the more fascinating. The confederate fortifications there offered yet another preview of the spring campaign, too.

At that same time, events unfolded in the West that had a significant impact in the East, but only when one looks at them in the context of each other does it become clear why. Grant's resounding success at Chattanooga compared to Meade's caution at Mine Run set the stage for Grant's ascension.

Following Mine Run, both armies encamped for the winter in pretty much the same areas they had begun the Bristoe campaign, spreading across dozens of square miles in Orange and Culpeper Counties. Hints of that fall and winter still remain on the landscape, but the story of those months has largely been erased. Bristoe Station Battlefield Heritage Park remains the single largest chunk of preserved land associated with that lost story.

That's why the work of Rob, Bill, and other historians, and the preservation efforts of groups like the Civil War Trust, remain vital. How can we remember a story if that story is literally wiped from the landscape?

GEN. LONGSTREET, C. S. A.

When the Confederates shifted Lt. Gen. James Longstreet (above) and his corps to the Western Theater, the Federals countered by shifting the XI and XII Corps west. Those movements inspired Lee and Meade to both take advantage of the new strategic situation on their front, thus leading to the Bristoe campaign. (loc)

CHRIS MACKOWSKI, PH.D., *is the editor-in-chief of Emerging Civil War*

HERE LIE MEN FROM
THE STATE OF ALABAMA

THESE MEN DIED FROM DISEASE INCURRED WHILE AT
CAMP JONES NEAR BRISTOE STATION AND
FROM NUMEROUS BATTLES IN NORTHERN VIRGINIA

AUGUST – DECEMBER 1861

"FAME'S TEMPLE BOASTS NO HIGHER NAME, NO KING IS GRANDER
ON HIS THRONE; NO GLORY SHINES WITH BRIGHTER GLEAM, THE
NAME OF "PATRIOT" STANDS ALONE."

# Chronology of Bristoe Station Preservation Efforts

## APPENDIX F

**1909**     James Coleman, veteran of the 10th Alabama Regiment, approaches Bristoe landowner in attempt to purchase the small space encompassing the 10th Alabama Cemetery. The owner, a daughter of a former Union soldier, declines but promises to protect the graves as long as she lives.

**1970s**     Battlefield land east of Bristow Rd. (Rt. 619) zoned for light industry.

**1988**     GLM Corp. purchases 256 acres of the rezoned land east of Rt. 619.

**Jan 1988**     County considers Bristow as site for new debris landfill.

**Feb 1988**     County drops Bristow as potential dump site due to opposition from both landowners & historians/preservationists citing the presence of Civil War graves. County gets a $10,000 grant to consider Bristow for inclusion on the National Register of Historic Places.

**Aug 1988**     County Archeologist Jan Townsend submits nomination for National Register.

The Alabama Cemetery includes the graves of nearly 100 Alabamians that died during the Summer-Fall 1861 at Camp Jones, located at Bristoe Station. The cemetery sits on the edge of the Bristoe Station Battlefield Heritage Park next to a housing development. It was part of the land saved in 2002. (cm)

**Nov 1988**     Virginia Division of Historic Landmarks drops designation
efforts due to strong landowner opposition.

**May 1989**     County (Jan Townsend) seeks historic overlay district for area,
which also meets with opposition from landowners.

**Jun 1990**     County removes Bristow for consideration as part of the
Cultural Resources element to the Comprehensive Plan
because it was not listed on the National Register or
recognized as a Virginia Historic Landmark. The "Save the
Battlefield Coalition" then resubmits the nomination to the
Dept. of Historic Resources without County support.

**Oct 1990**     State Review Board approves Bristow as eligible for listing on
the National Register. Action to place Bristow on the state's
Historic Landmarks Register is deferred at the request of
County officials.

**Apr 1991**     Despite continued landowner opposition, the Virginia Dept. of
Historic Resources places Bristow on the Virginia Landmarks
Register.

**Jan 1992**     Virginia General Assembly passes SB514, changing the rules
for state historic designations to require the consent of a
majority of landowners (as required for listing on National
Register). Law is made retroactive to cause reconsideration of
Bristow and Brandy Station.

**May 1993**     Virginia Dept. of Historic Resources removes state landmark
designation for Bristow. The County initiates Comprehensive
Plan Amendment 93-018 for Bristow Station battlefield.

**Oct 1993**     County Planning staff submits report to the Planning
Commission for review & approval. Plan includes various
action strategies to mitigate development impacts to cultural
resources. Planning Commission defers action to consider
several alternatives submitted by landowners' representative
(all higher density plans).

**Modern day development surrounds the Bristoe Station Battlefield Heritage Park on two sides. Only 25% of the Bristoe Station battlefield is preserved today.** (ro)

**Feb 1994**    Planning Commission overwhelmingly approves "Alternative 1" (the original staff recommendation) and rejects the higher density plans.

**May 1994**    Brentsville Supervisor William Becker requests deferral by the Board of Supervisors so that he can work out a "compromise" alternative.

**Jun 1994**    Board of Supervisors approves Mr. Becker's "Alternative 7," which allows the highest densities with the option of clustered housing and encourages easements for public access trails in areas that cannot otherwise be developed.

**Jun 1994**    The 256 acres purchased in 1988 by GLM Corp. (now bankrupt) is sold at auction for $700,000 to Pete Ebert & Associates. Initially unable to raise the needed capital, this partnership is later reorganized in August as the "Broad Run L.C." and title is finally transferred.

In 2007, the Civil War Trust deeded over 127 acres to Prince William County to form the Bristoe Station Battlefield Heritage Park. Sean T. Connaughton, Chairman of the Prince William Board of County Supervisors, and James Lighthizer, president of the Civil War Trust, signed the deal. (pwc)

**Dec 1994**   County Historical Commission approaches the Broad Run L.C. seeking permission to conduct a search for unmarked graves on their property before any plans for development are made. Doug Owsley, forensic anthropologist with the Smithsonian, would head the project. Permission is never obtained.

**Dec 1996**   County Historical Commission submits a grant application to the American Battlefield Protection Program (administered by NPS) for the purpose of developing action strategies for identifying and preserving key battlefield resources at Bristow. A $10,000 grant is awarded in 1997, but the County rejects it for lack of sufficient staff to administer the grant.

**1997**   The Broad Run L.C. property is subdivided and sold to the Manassas Assembly of God (155 acres) and a "Golf Academy" (99 acres). Phase I archeological survey reports are completed by Thunderbird Archeological Associates. Historical Commission review finds numerous flaws in both reports.

**1998**          Manassas Assembly of God receives rezoning approval for
                 construction of a massive church facility on 37 acres. The
                 potential for unmarked graves on the property is brought up in
                 rezoning hearings.

**Dec 2000**     Centex Homes becomes the contract purchaser of the 341-
                 acre Rollins tract on the west side of Rt. 619 with plans for
                 "New Bristow Village." Centex applies for rezoning (PLN
                 2001-00157). Thunderbird Archeological Associates completes
                 a Phase I study acknowledging the potential for unmarked
                 graves on the tract.

**Jun 2001**     Thermal-imaging survey sponsored by the Sons of Confederate
                 Veterans identifies another possible cemetery (44PW1234) in
                 woods east of the 10th Alabama Cemetery. Centex tentatively
                 offers 127 acres in the core of the Bristoe Station battlefield to
                 the Civil War Preservation Trust (CWPT).

**Oct 2001**     Centex submits proffers to County to include the donation of
                 127 acres to the CWPT as a quid-pro-quo for higher density
                 housing elsewhere on the tract. The only provision addressing
                 unmarked graves is having an archeologist monitor grading
                 operations.

**Feb 2002**     County Planning Commission approves Centex plan.
                 Historical Commission supports the rezoning but recommends
                 an independent survey for unmarked graves before land
                 disturbance.

**Mar 2002**     Board of Supervisors approves Centex rezoning after Centex
                 amends proffers to fund GPR study in a 50' buffer around the
                 known cemeteries. Centex also agrees to allow access for an
                 independent survey for a 120-day period.

**Feb 2003**     Norfolk-Southern Railroad begins land clearing for a new crew
                 change station along Milford Rd. in the Northeast quadrant of
                 the battlefield. Archeological monitoring for unmarked graves
                 is subverted by the worst possible ground conditions.

Although primarily preserved because of its historical value, the Bristoe battlefield has become an important green space in the middle of commercial and residential development. Wildlife and wild flowers comprise a vibrant ecosystem, which nature lovers can enjoy thanks to the park's trail system. (cm)

**July 2003**    Centex takes title to the Rollins tract and the independent archeological survey begins. This survey, sponsored by the Sons of Confederate Veterans, headed by archeologist Patrick O'Neill, and completed in November 2003, has negative results. No additional unmarked graves were located in areas planned for development.

**Sep 2004**    Centex transfers title of 127 acres to the CWPT, although construction activities (sewer/utility lines, storm water overflow) continue to negatively impact the "saved" acreage. CWPT begins planning trail network and historical markers (contracting Mike Miller) with intent to ultimately transfer the acreage to Prince William County.

**Mar 2006**    Rezoning # 2006-00498 for a 155-acre business park threatens to impact Union artillery positions in the southeast quadrant of the battlefield. Plans for a communications monopole along the railroad also threaten the battlefield viewshed.

**Jun 27, 2006**  CWPT officially transfers their Bristoe battlefield land, now expanded to 133 acres, to the Historic Preservation Division of the Prince William County Dept. of Public Works. Bristoe Station Battlefield Heritage Park is thus created.

**Oct 12, 2007**  Dedication ceremony for Bristoe Station Battlefield Heritage Park. With parking area and trails completed, the park grounds are officially opened to the public.

**Mar 19, 2008**  County Planning Commission hearing to consider rezoning for "Manassas Business Park" in southeast quadrant of the battlefield to include position of Ricketts's battery. County planning staff report and Historical Commission recommend denial of application due to negative impact on the battlefield.

**May 6, 2008**  Board of Supervisors approves rezoning for the Manassas Business Park after the applicant proffered 42 acres to the county for addition to the Bristoe Station Battlefield Heritage Park (expanding the park to 175 total acres). This amended plan gained the support of the Planning staff, Historical Commission, Bull Run CWRT representatives, and CWPT.

**Spring 2013**  Chapel Springs Assembly of God (formerly Manassas Assembly of God), propose a commercial cemetery over their land where Brig. Gen. William Kirkland's brigade made their assault on October 14, 1863. Bull Run Civil War Roundtable, County Historical Commission, CWPT and other local groups voice concerns and call for a preservation-friendly compromise. Bristoe Station battlefield is listed as a Top Ten Most Endangered Site by Preservation Virginia.

**May 2014**  James Robeson donates seven adjacent acres to Prince William County for inclusion in the Bristoe Station Battlefield Heritage Park.

Timeline created with
assistance from Jim Burgess,
Prince William County
Historical Commission.

# Order of Battle

## ARMY OF THE POTOMAC
Maj. Gen. George Gordon Meade

**Provost Guard:** Brig. Gen. Marsena Patrick
*80th New York (20th Militia)* • *93rd New York* • *2nd Pennsylvania Cavalry* •
*Detachment 6th Pennsylvania Cavalry*
**Engineer Brigade:** Brig. Gen. Henry Benham
*15th New York Engineers* • *50th New York Engineers* • *United States
Engineer Battalion*

**FIRST ARMY CORPS:** Maj. Gen. John Newton
**Headquarters Escort:** *Detachment 4th and 16th Pennsylvania Cavalry*

**FIRST DIVISION:** Brig. Gen. Lysander Cutler
**First Brigade (Iron Brigade):** Col. William Robinson
*19th Indiana* • *24th Michigan* • *1st New York Sharpshooters*
*2nd Wisconsin* • *6th Wisconsin* • *7th Wisconsin*
**Second Brigade:** Brig. Gen. James Rice
*7th Indiana* • *76th New York* • *84th New York (14th Militia)*
*95th New York* • *147th New York* • *56th Pennsylvania*

**SECOND DIVISION:** Brig. Gen. John. Robinson
**First Brigade:** Col. Thomas McCoy
*16th Maine* • *13th Massachusetts* • *39th Massachusetts*
*94th New York* • *104th New York* • *107th Pennsylvania*

**Second Brigade:** Brig. Gen. Henry Baxter
*12th Massachusetts* • *83rd New York (9th Militia)* • *97th New York*
*11th Pennsylvania* • *88th Pennsylvania* • *90th Pennsylvania*

**THIRD DIVISION:** Brig. Gen. John Kenly
**First Brigade:** Col. Chapman Biddle
*121st Pennsylvania* • *142nd Pennsylvania*

**Second Brigade (Bucktail Brigade):** Col. Langhorne Wister
*143rd Pennsylvania* • *149th Pennsylvania* • *150th Pennsylvania*

**Third Brigade:** Col. Nathan Dushane
*1st Maryland  •  4th Maryland  •  7th Maryland  •  8th Maryland*

**Corps Artillery:** Col. Charles Wainwright
*2nd Battery, Maine Light  •  5th Battery, Maine Light*
*Batteries E & L, 1st Pennsylvania Light  •  Battery B, 4th United States*

**SECOND ARMY CORPS**: Maj. Gen. Gouverneur Warren
**Escort:** *Company M, 10th New York Cavalry*
*Company G, 13th Pennsylvania Cavalry*

**FIRST DIVISION:** Brig. Gen. John Caldwell
**First Brigade:** Col. Nelson Miles
*61st New York  •  81st Pennsylvania  •  140th Pennsylvania*

**Second Brigade** (Irish Brigade): Col. Patrick Kelly
*28th Massachusetts  •  63rd New York  •  69th New York*
*88th New York  •  116th Pennsylvania*

**Third Brigade:** Col. James Beaver
*52nd New York  •  57th New York  •  66th New York  •  148th Pennsylvania*

**Fourth Brigade:** Col. John Brooke
*2nd Delaware  •  64th New York  •  53rd Pennsylvania  •  145th Pennsylvania*

**SECOND DIVISION:** Brig. Gen. Alexander Webb
**First Brigade:** Col. Francis Heath
*19th Maine  •  15th Massachusetts  •  1st Minnesota*
*82nd New York (2nd Militia)*

**Second Brigade (Philadelphia Brigade):** Col. De Witt Baxter
*69th Pennsylvania  •  71st Pennsylvania  •  72nd Pennsylvania*
*06th Pennsylvania*

**Third Brigade**: Col. James Mallon
*19th Massachusetts  •  20th Massachusetts  •  7th Michigan*
*42nd New York  •  59th New York*

**THIRD DIVISION:** Brig. Gen. Alexander Hays
**First Brigade** (Gibraltar Brigade): Samuel Carroll
*14th Indiana  •  4th Ohio  •  8th Ohio  •  7th West Virginia*

**Second Brigade:** Col. Thomas Smyth
*14th Connecticut  •  1st Delaware  •  12th New Jersey*
*10th New York (battalion)  •  108th New York*

**Third Brigade:** Brig. Gen. Joshua Owen
*39th New York  •  111th New York  •  125th New York  •  126th New York*

**Corps Artillery:** Capt. John Hazard
*Battery G, 1st New York Light • Battery H, 1st Ohio Light*
*Batteries F& G, 1st Pennsylvania Light • Battery A, 1st Rhode Island Light*
*Battery B, 1st Rhode Island Light • Battery I, 1st United States*


**THRID CORPS:** Maj. Gen. William French
**FIRST DIVISION:** Maj. Gen. David Birney
**First Brigade:** Col. Charles Collis
*57th Pennsylvania • 63rd Pennsylvania • 68th Pennsylvania*
*105th Pennsylvania • 114th Pennsylvania • 141st Pennsylvania*

**Second Brigade:** Brig. Gen. J. H. Hobart Ward
*3rd Maine • 4th Maine • 86th New York • 124th New York*
*99th Pennsylvania • 2nd U.S. Sharpshooters*

**Third Brigade**: Col. Regis De Trobriand
*17th Maine • 3rd Michigan • 5th Michigan • 40th New York*
*110th Pennsylvania • 1st U.S. Sharpshooters*

**SECOND DIVISION:** Brig. Gen. Henry Prince
**First Brigade:** Col. Robert McAllister
*11th Massachusetts • 16th Massachusetts • 11th New Jersey*
*26th Pennsylvania • 84th Pennsylvania*

**Second Brigade** (Excelsior Brigade): Col. William Brewster
*70th New York • 71st New York • 72nd New York • 73rd New York*
*74th New York • 120th New York*

**Third Brigade** (Second New Jersey Brigade): Brig. Gen. Gershom Mott
*5th New Jersey • 6th New Jersey • 7th New Jersey • 8th New Jersey*
*115th Pennsylvania*

**THIRD DIVISION**: Brig. Gen. Joseph Carr
First Brigade: Brig. Gen. William Morris
*14th New Jersey • 151st New York • 10th Vermont*

**Second Brigade:** J. Warren Keifer
*6th Maryland • 110th Ohio • 122nd Ohio • 138th Pennsylvania*

**Third Brigade:** Col. Benjamin Smith
*106th New York • 126th Ohio • 67th Pennsylvania • 87th Pennsylvania*

**Corps Artillery**: Capt. George Randolph
*4th Battery, Maine Light • 10th Battery, Massachusetts Light • Battery B, New Jersey Light • Battery D, 1st New York Light • 12th Battery, New York Light Battery E, 1st Rhode Island Light • Battery K, 4th United States*

**FIFTH CORPS:** Maj. Gen. George Sykes
**Escort:** Detachment 5th Michigan Cavalry
Provost Guard: Companies D & E, 12th New York
**FIRST DIVISION**: Brig. Gen. Charles Griffin
**First Brigade**: Brig. Gen. James Barnes
*18th Massachusetts • 22nd Massachusetts • 1st Michigan • 118th Pennsylvania*

**Second Brigade:** Col. Jacob Sweitzer
*9th Massachusetts • 32nd Massachusetts • 4th Michigan • 62nd Pennsylvania*

**Third Brigade**: Col. Joshua Chamberlain
*20th Maine • 16th Michigan • 44th New York • 83rd Pennsylvania*

**SECOND DIVISION:** Brig. Gen. Romeyn Ayres
**First Brigade: Col. Sidney Burbank**
*2nd United States (six companies) • 3rd United States (six companies)
11th United States • 12th United States • 14th United States
17th United States*

**Third Brigade:** Brig. Gen. Kenner Garrard
*140th New York • 146th New York • 91st Pennsylvania
155th Pennsylvania*

**THIRD DIVISION**: Col. William McCandless
**First Brigade**: Col. William Talley
*1st Pennsylvania Reserves • 2nd Pennsylvania Reserves
6th Pennsylvania Reserves • 13th Pennsylvania Reserves*

**Third Brigade**: Col. Martin Hardin
*5th Pennsylvania Reserves • 9th Pennsylvania Reserves
10th Pennsylvania Reserves • 11th Pennsylvania Reserves
12th Pennsylvania Reserves*

**Corps Artillery:** Capt. Augustus Martin
*3rd Battery, Massachusetts Light • 5th Battery, Massachusetts Light
Battery C, 1st New York Light • Battery L, 1st Ohio Light
Battery D, 5th United States*

**SIXTH CORPS**: Maj. Gen. John Sedgwick
**Escort:** Detachment 1st Vermont Cavalry
**FIRST DIVISION:** Brig. Gen. Horatio Wright
**First Brigade (First New Jersey Brigade):** Brig. Gen. Alfred Torbert
*1st New Jersey • 2nd New Jersey • 3rd New Jersey • 4th New Jersey
15th New Jersey*

**Second Brigade:** Brig. Gen. Joseph Bartlett
*5th Maine • 121st New York • 95th Pennsylvania • 96th Pennsylvania*

**Third Brigade**: Brig. Gen. David Russell
*6th Maine • 49th Pennsylvania • 119th Pennsylvania • 5th Wisconsin*

**SECOND DIVISION:** Brig. Gen. Albion Howe
**Second Brigade (Vermont Brigade):** Col. Lewis Grant
*2nd Vermont • 3rd Vermont • 4th Vermont • 5th Vermont • 6th Vermont*

**Third Brigade:** Brig. Gen. Thomas Neill
*7th Maine • 43rd New York • 49th New York • 77th New York
61st Pennsylvania*

**THIRD DIVISION:** Brig. Gen. Henry Terry
**First Brigade:** Brig. Gen. Alexander Shaler
*65th New York • 67th New York • 122nd New York
23rd Pennsylvania • 82nd Pennsylvania*

**Second Brigade:** Brig. Gen. Henry Eustis
*7th Massachusetts • 10th Massachusetts • 2nd Rhode Island*

**Third Brigade:** Brig. Gen. Frank Wheaton
*62nd New York • 93rd Pennsylvania • 98th Pennsylvania
102nd Pennsylvania • 139th Pennsylvania*

**Corps Artillery:** Col. Charles Tompkins
*1st Battery, Massachusetts Light • 1st Battery, New York Light
3rd Battery, New York Light • Battery C, 1st Rhode Island Light
Battery G, 1st Rhode Island Light • Battery F, 5th United States
Battery M, 5th United States*


**CAVALRY CORPS**: Maj. Gen. Alfred Pleasonton
*Headquarters Guard: 6th United States*

**FIRST DIVISION**: Brig. Gen. John Buford
First Brigade: Col. George Chapman
*8th Illinois Cavalry • 12th Illinois Cavalry • 3rd Indiana Cavalry
8th New York Cavalry*

**Second Brigade:** Col. Thomas Devin
*4th New York Cavalry • 6th New York Cavalry • 9th New York Cavalry
17th Pennsylvania Cavalry • 3rd West Virginia Cavalry*

**SECOND DIVISION:** Brig. Gen. David Gregg
**First Brigade:** Col. John Taylor
*1st Maryland Cavalry • 1st Massachusetts Cavalry • 1st New Jersey Cavalry
6th Ohio Cavalry • 1st Pennsylvania Cavalry • 3rd Pennsylvania Cavalry
1st Rhode Island Cavalry*

**Second Brigade:** Col. Irvin Gregg
*District of Columbia, Independent Company* · *1st Maine Cavalry* · *10th New York Cavalry* · *4th Pennsylvania Cavalry* · *8th Pennsylvania Cavalry* · *13th Pennsylvania Cavalry* · *16th Pennsylvania Cavalry*

**THIRD DIVISION:** Brig. Gen. Judson Kilpatrick
Headquarters Guard: Companies A & C, 1st Ohio Cavalry
**First Brigade:** Brig. Gen. Henry Davies, Jr.
*2nd New York Cavalry* · *5th New York Cavalry*
*18th Pennsylvania Cavalry* · *1st West Virginia Cavalry*

**Second Brigade (Michigan Brigade):** Brig. Gen. George Custer
*1st Michigan Cavalry* · *5th Michigan Cavalry* · *6th Michigan Cavalry*
*7th Michigan Cavalry* · *1st Vermont Cavalry*

**Reserve Brigade:** Brig. Gen. Wesley Merrit
*6th Pennsylvania Cavalry* · *1st United States Cavalry*
*2nd United States Cavalry* · *5th United States Cavalry*

**Unattached:**
*19th New York (1st Dragoons)*

**RESERVE ARTILLERY:** Brig. Gen. Robert Tyler
**First Regular Brigade:** Capt. Alanson Randol
*Battery H, 1st United States* · *Batteries F & K, 3rd United States*
*Battery C, 4th United States*

**First Volunteer Brigade:** Lt. Col. Freeman McGilvery
*6th Battery, Maine Light* · *9th Battery, Massachusetts Light*
*4th Battery, New York Light* · *Batteries C & F, Pennsylvania Light*

**Second Volunteer Brigade:** Capt. Elijah Taft
*Battery B, 1st Connecticut Heavy* · *Battery M, 1st Connecticut Heavy*
*Battery B, 1st New York Light* · *5th Battery, New York Light*
*Battery C, West Virginia Light*

**Third Volunteer Brigade:** Maj. Robert Fitzhugh
*Battery A, Maryland Light* · *1st Battery, New Hampshire Light*
*Battery A, New Jersey Light* · *Battery K, 1st New York Light*
*15th Battery, New York Light*

**First Brigade** Horse Artillery: Capt. James Robertson
*6th Battery, New York Light* · *Batteries B & L, 2nd United States*
*Battery D, 2nd United States* · *Battery M, 2nd United States*
*Battery A, 4th United States* · *Battery E, 4th United States*

**Second Brigade Horse Artillery:** Capt. William Graham
*9th Battery, Michigan Light* · *Battery K, 1st United State* · *Battery K, 1st United States* · *Battery A, 2nd United States* · *Battery G, 2nd United States* · *Battery C, 3rd United States*

**Ammunition Guard:**
*8th New York Heavy Artillery*

# ARMY OF NORTHERN VIRGINIA
## Gen. Robert E. Lee

**SECOND CORPS**: Lt. Gen. Richard Ewell
**EARLY'S DIVISION:** Maj. Gen. Jubal Early
**Hays's Brigade**: Brig. Gen. Henry Hays
*5th Louisiana • 6th Louisiana • 7th Louisiana • 8th Louisiana
9th Louisiana*

**Gordon's Brigade:** Brig. Gen. John Gordon
*13th Georgia • 26th Georgia • 31st Georgia • 38th Georgia
60th Georgia • 61st Georgia*

**Hoke's Brigade:** Col. Archibald Godwin
*6th North Carolina • 21st North Carolina • 54th North Carolina
57th North Carolina • 1st North Carolina Battalion Sharpshooters*

**Smith's Brigade:** Brig. Gen. John Pegram
*13th Virginia • 31st Virginia • 49th Virginia • 52nd Virginia • 58th Virginia*

**JOHNSON'S DIVISION:** Maj. Gen. Edward Johnson
**Stonewall Brigade:** Brig. Gen. James Walker
*2nd Virginia • 4th Virginia • 5th Virginia • 27th Virginia • 33rd Virginia*

**Jones's Brigade:** Brig. Gen. John Jones
*21st Virginia • 25th Virginia • 42nd Virginia • 44th Virginia
48th Virginia • 50th Virginia*

**Steuart's Brigade:** Brig. Gen. George Steuart
*1st Maryland Battalion • 1st North Carolina • 3rd North Carolina
10th Virginia • 23rd Virginia • 37th Virginia*

**Stafford's Brigade:** Brig. Gen. Leroy Stafford
*1st Louisiana • 2nd Louisiana • 10th Louisiana • 14th Louisiana
15th Louisiana*

**RODES'S DIVISION**: Maj. Gen. Robert Rodes
**Daniel's Brigade:** Brig. Gen. Junius Daniel
*32nd North Carolina • 43rd North Carolina • 45th North Carolina
53rd North Carolina • 2nd North Carolina Battalion*

**Doles's Brigade:** Brig. Gen. George Doles
*4th Georgia • 12th Georgia • 21st Georgia • 44th Georgia*

**Ramseur's Brigade:** Brig. Gen. Stephen Ramseur
*2nd North Carolina • 4th North Carolina • 14th North Carolina
30th North Carolina*

**Battle's Brigade:** Brig. Gen. Cullen Battle
*3rd Alabama* • *5th Alabama* • *6th Alabama*
*12th Alabama* • *26th Alabama*

**Johnston's Brigade:** Col. Thomas Garrett
*5th North Carolina* • *12th North Carolina* • *20th North Carolina*
*23rd North Carolina*

**SECOND CORPS ARTILLERY:** Brig. Gen. Armistead Long
*First Regiment Virginia Artillery: Col. J. Thompson Brown*
*2nd Richmond (Virginia) Howitzers* • *3rd Richmond (Virginia) Howitzers*
*Powhatan (Virginia) Artillery* • *Rockbridge (Virginia) Artillery*
*Salem (Virginia) Flying Artillery*

**Andrews's Battalion:** Lt. Col. Richard Andrews
*1st Maryland Artillery* • *Chesapeake (Maryland) Artillery*
*Alleghany (Virginia) Artillery* • *Lee (Virginia) Battery*

**Nelson's Battalion:** Lt. Col. William Nelson
*Milledge's (Georgia) Battery* • *Amherst (Virginia) Artillery*
*Fluvanna (Virginia) Artillery*

**Jones's Battalion:** Lt. Col. Hilary Jones
*Louisiana Guard Artillery* • *Charlottesville (Virginia) Artillery*
*Courtney (Virginia) Artillery* • *Staunton (Virginia) Artillery*

**Carter's Battalion:** Lt. Col. Thomas Carter
*Jefferson Davis (Alabama) Artillery* • *King William (Virginia) Artillery*
*Morris (Virginia) Artillery* • *Orange (Virginia) Artillery*

**THIRD CORPS**: Lt. Gen. A. P. Hill
**ANDERSONS' DIVISION**: Maj. Gen. Richard Anderson
**Wilcox's Brigade:** Col. John Sanders
*8th Alabama* • *9th Alabama* • *10th Alabama* • *11th Alabama*
*14th Alabama*

**Mahone's Brigade**: Brig. Gen. William Mahone
*6th Virginia* • *12th Virginia* • *16th Virginia* • *41st Virginia* • *61st Virginia*

**Posey's Brigade:** Brig. Gen. Carnot Posey
*12th Mississippi* • *16th Mississippi* • *19th Mississippi* • *48th Mississippi*

**Wright's Brigade:** Brig. Gen. Ambrose Wright
*3rd Georgia* • *22nd Georgia* • *48th Georgia* • *2nd Georgia Battalion*

**Perry's Brigade**: Brig. Gen. Edward Perry
*2nd Florida* • *5th Florida* • *8th Florida*

**HETH'S DIVISION**: Maj. Gen. Henry Heth
**Davis's Brigade:** Brig. Gen. Joseph Davis
*2nd Mississippi* • *11th Mississippi* • *42nd Mississippi* • *55th North Carolina*

**Walker's Brigade:** Brig. Gen. Henry Walker
*5th Alabama Battalion* • *13th Alabama* • *1st Tennessee* • *7th Tennessee 14th Tennessee* • *40th Virginia* • *47th Virginia* • *55th Virginia* • *22nd Virginia Battalion*

**Kirkland's Brigade:** Brig. Gen. William Kirkland
*11th North Carolina* • *26th North Carolina* • *44th North Carolina 47th North Carolina* • *52nd North Carolina*

**Cooke's Brigade:** Brig. Gen. John Cooke
*15th North Carolina* • *27th North Carolina* • *46th North Carolina 48th North Carolina*

**WILCOX'S DIVISION**: Maj. Gen. Cadmus Wilcox
**Lane's Brigade:** Brig. Gen. James Lane
*7th North Carolina* • *18th North Carolina* • *28th North Carolina 33rd North Carolina* • *37th North Carolina*

**Thomas's Brigade:** Brig. Gen. Edward Thomas
*14th Georgia* • *35th Georgia* • *45th Georgia* • *49th Georgia*

**McGowan's Brigade:** Brig. Gen. Abner Perrin
*1st South Carolina (Provisional Army)* • *12th South Carolina 3th South Carolina* • *14th South Carolina* • *Orr's (South Carolina) Rifles*

**Scales's Brigade:** Alfred Scales
*13th North Carolina* • *16th North Carolina* • *22nd North Carolina 34th North Carolina* • *38th North Carolina*

**THIRD CORPS ARTILLERY**: Col. R. Lindsay Walker
**Sumter Artillery:** Lt. Col. Allen Cutts
*Irwin (Georgia) Battery, Patterson's (Georgia) Battery, Ross's (Georgia) Battery*

**Garnett's Battalion:** Lt. Col. John Garnett
*Donaldsonville (Louisiana) Artillery* • *Moore's Company (Virginia) Artillery Lewis (Virginia) Artillery* • *Norfolk (Virginia) Blues Artillery*

**McIntosh's Battalion:** Maj. David McIntosh
*Hardaway (Alabama) Artillery* • *Danville (Virginia) Artillery Johnson's (Virginia) Battery* •
*2nd Rockbridge (Virginia) Artillery*

**Pegram's Battalion**: Maj. William Pegram
*Pee Dee (South Carolina) Artillery* • *Crenshaw (Virginia) Battery Fredericksburg (Virginia) Artillery* • *Letcher (Virginia) Artillery* • *Purcell (Virginia) Artillery*

**Poague's Battalion:** Lt. Col William Poague
*Madison (Mississippi) Artillery  •  Graham's (North Carolina) Artillery*
*Albemarle (Virginia) Artillery  •  Brooke's (Virginia) Battery*


**CAVALRY CORPS:** Maj. Gen. J. E. B. Stuart
**HAMPTON'S DIVISION:** Maj. Gen. J. E. B. Stuart
**Gordon's Brigade:** Brig. Gen. James B. Gordon
*1st North Carolina Cavalry  •  2nd North Carolina Cavalry*
*4th North Carolina Cavalry  •  5th North Carolina Cavalry*

**Butler's Brigade**: Brig. Gen. Pierce Young
*1st South Carolina Cavalry  •  2nd South Carolina Cavalry*
*Cobb's (Georgia) Legion  •  Phillips (Georgia) Legion*
*Jeff Davis (Mississippi) Legion*

**Jones's Brigade:** Col. Oliver Funsten
*7th Virginia Cavalry  •  11th Virginia Cavalry  •  12th Virginia Cavalry*

**FITZHUGH LEE'S DIVISION:** Maj. Gen. Fitzhugh Lee
**Lee's Brigade:** Col. John Chambliss, Jr.
*9th Virginia Cavalry  •  10th Virginia Cavalry  •  13th Virginia Cavalry*

**Lomax's Brigade:** Brig. Gen. Lunsford Lomax
*1st Maryland Cavalry Battalion  •  5th Virginia Cavalry*
*6th Virginia Cavalry  •  15th Virginia Cavalry*

**Wickham's Brigade:** Col. Thomas Owen
*1st Virginia Cavalry  •  2nd Virginia Cavalry  •  3rd Virginia Cavalry*
*4th Virginia Cavalry*

**ARTILLERY SERVING WITH CAVALRY CORPS**: Maj. Robert Beckham
*Breathed's (Virginia) Battery  •  Chew's (Virginia) Battery*
*Griffin's (Maryland) Battery  •  Hart's (South Carolina) Battery*
*McGregor's (Virginia) Battery  •  Moorman's (Virginia) Battery*


**ARTILLERY RESERVE**
**Cabell's Battalion:** Col. Henry Cabell
*Fraser's (Georgia) Battery  •  Troup (Georgia) Artillery*
*Manly's (North Carolina) Battery  •  1st Richmond (Virginia) Howitzers*

**Haskell's Battalion:** Maj. John Haskell
*Branch (North Carolina) Artillery  •  Rowan (North Carolina) Artillery*
*Palmetto South Carolina Artillery*

# Suggested Reading

*The Maps of the Bristoe Station
and Mine Run Campaigns*
Bradley Gottfried
Savas Beatie, 2013
ISBN-13: 978-1611211528

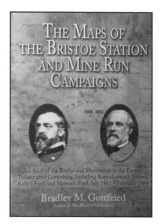

The Bristoe Station edition of Brad Gottfried's
popular map book provides clear maps and
informative interpretive text. The maps allow the
reader to follow along the vast territory that both
armies marched across central Virginia. The book
also explains the actions in September that led up
to the Bristoe campaign.

*The Road to Bristoe Station*
William D. Henderson
H.E. Howard, 1987
ISBN: 0930919459 9780930919450

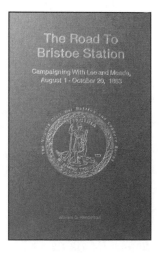

For a long time, this was the only published work
on the Bristoe Station campaign. Focusing mostly
on the campaign more than the battle, Henderson's
work set the stage for all other published materials
on the campaign.

*The Bristoe Campaign*
Adrian G. Tighe
Xlibris, 2011
ISBN-13: 978-1456888688

Adrian Tighe's study on the Bristoe Station campaign was its first study in more than 20 years. The author includes an immense amount of research and, with new sources, reinterprets several portions of the campaign and battle. Tighe also puts the events in Virginia into context of events planned by the Confederate leadership in the fall of 1863.

*After Gettysburg: Cavalry Operations in the Eastern Theater,*
*July 14, 1863 – December 31, 1863*
Robert Trout
Eagle Editions, 2012
ISBN-13: 978-0979403576

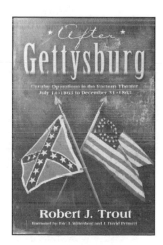

The cavalry did the brunt of the fighting and movement during the Bristoe Station campaign, and Robert Trout focuses on the importance of the mounted arm during the fall campaign. This book covers all cavalry actions after Gettysburg before the Overland Campaign, but focuses a substantial portion on the October campaign.

# About the Authors

## Robert Orrison

Rob Orrison has been working in the history field for more than 20 years. Born and raised in Loudoun County, Virginia, Rob received his bachelor's degree in Historic Preservation at Longwood College (now University) and received his master's degree in Public History from George Mason University. Currently Rob oversees day-to-day operations of a large municipal historic site program in Northern Virginia. Outside of work, Rob leads tours with Civil War Excursion Tours (of which he is co-founder), contributor to the Emerging Civil War blog, and treasurer of the Historic House Museum Consortium of Washington, D.C. He serves as a member of the board of directors of the Bull Run Civil War Roundtable, the board of directors of the Mosby Heritage Area Association, the board of directors of Virginia Civil War Trails, and serves on the Governing Council of the Virginia Association of Museums. He lives in Prince William County with his wife, Jamie, and son, Carter.

## Bill Backus

A native of Connecticut, Bill Backus graduated from the University of Mary Washington with a bachelor's degree in Historic Preservation. Currently working as a historian for multiple Civil War sites in Northern Virginia, Bill has worked for the National Park Service at Vicksburg National Military Park and Petersburg National Battlefield. Bill currently resides in historic Brentsville, Virginia, with his wife, Paige, and their dog, Barley.